Englische Grammatik
9./10. Schuljahr

32 Arbeitsblätter
für einen kommunikativen Grammatikunterricht

von Margaret und Detlef von Ziegésar

Ernst Klett Verlag
Stuttgart München Düsseldorf Leipzig

Abbildungsnachweise:

S. 21: Rudolf Klem, Stuttgart; S. 31: British Tourist Authority, Frankfurt/Karin Klem, Stuttgart; S. 32: British Tourist Authority, Frankfurt/Karin Klem, Stuttgart/„The Sun" News International, London; S. 59: foto-present, Essen; S.88: Zeichnung der Autorin

Gedruckt auf Papier, welches aus Altpapier hergestellt wurde.

Die Deutsche Bibliothek – CIP-Einheitsaufnahme

Ziegésar, Margaret von:
Englische Grammatik 9./10. Schuljahr :
32 Arbeitblätter für einen kommunikativen Grammatikunterricht /
von Margaret von Ziegésar und Detlef von Ziegésar. –
1. Aufl. – Stuttgart ; München ; Düsseldorf ; Leipzig : Klett 1996
ISBN 3-12-927884-2

1. Auflage 1996

Umschlaggestaltung: BSS Werbeagentur Sachse und Partner, Bietigheim
Illustrationen: Christa Janik, Leinfelden-Echterdingen
Druck und Bindung: Wilhelm Röck, Weinsberg
Printed in Germany.
ISBN 3-12-927884-2

Adverbien

Allgemeines

Dies ist das dritte Arbeitsbuch zur Übung und Wiederholung von Grammatikstrukturen im Englischunterricht der Sekundarstufe I. Der vorliegende dritte Band umfaßt das Grammatikpensum der Klassen 9 und 10, der erste Band enthält die in den Klassen 5 und 6 behandelten Grammatikstrukturen, der zweite Band übt und wiederholt das Grammatikpensum der Klassen 7 und 8.
Der erste Teil der einzelnen Bände enthält für jede behandelte Grammatikstruktur sorgfältig durchdachte und im Unterricht erprobte Arbeitsblätter. Der zweite Teil stellt detaillierte und übersichtliche didaktisch-methodische Hinweise samt Lösungsvorschläge zu den Übungen für die Hand der Lehrkraft bereit.
Die Arbeitsblätter können sowohl im Verbund mit einem Lehrwerk als auch lehrbuchunabhängig verwendet werden. Der Wortschatz sowie die Progression der grammatischen Strukturen korrespondieren mit denen der gängigen Englischlehrwerke.
Man kann die Arbeitsbücher in der vorgegebenen Reihenfolge der Strukturen systematisch durchgehen, aber auch je nach Bedarf einzelne Grammatikphänomene herausgreifen.
Die Arbeitsblätter enthalten sowohl mündliche als auch schriftliche Übungen und berücksichtigen die verschiedenen Sozialformen des Unterrichts. Dadurch ist der Einsatz der Arbeitsblätter vielfältig. Es gibt lehrergelenkte Übungen, Gruppen-, Partner- und Projektarbeit. Einzelarbeit ist sowohl in der Klasse als auch zu Hause in Form von Hausaufgaben möglich.

Grammatik

Der vorliegende Band übt und wiederholt die wichtigsten Grammatikphänomone der Klassen 9 und 10 mit strukturierten Materialien in Form von Arbeitsblättern.
Die Arbeitsblätter sind einerseits nach formalgrammatischen Gesichtspunkten geordnet und folgen damit der von den Lehrplänen der verschiedenen Bundesländer vorgeschriebenen und in Lehrwerken verwirklichten Strukturenprogression. Andererseits betten sie die zu übenden Grammatikstrukturen in natürliche Kommunikationssituationen ein und wählen den Strukturen angemessene Textsorten und Themen. Dadurch ist sowohl ein formalgrammatisches Üben und Einschleifen, als auch ein kommunikatives Verwenden der Strukturen gewährleistet.
Obwohl der Schwerpunkt der Arbeitsblätter auf dem Üben und Wiederholen von Grammatikstrukturen liegt, werden immer wieder Gelegenheiten zum induktiven Erarbeiten von Grammatikregeln geboten, und Regeln werden, wenn notwendig, in übersichtlichen Merkkästchen zusammengefaßt. Die Regeln sind auf deutsch und in einer schülernahen Sprache verfaßt, die den Lernenden vermittelt, daß Regeln nicht um ihrer selbst willen zu lernen sind, sondern als Hilfsmittel zum Erlernen der fremden Sprache.

Textsorten, Themen und Sozialformen

Soweit wie möglich wird mit sprachlich zwar vereinfachten, aber authentischen Textsorten gearbeitet. Es kommen informative Sachtexte vor, Erzähltexte, Werbetexte, Zeitungsannoncen, Hinweisschilder, Briefe und ein Wetterbericht. Die Schüler üben und wiederholen in dieser Weise Grammatikstrukturen mit Hilfe von Texten, die ihnen glaubwürdig erscheinen und denen sie in der Realität begegnen können.
Die Themen sind schülernah, indem sie die Erfahrungs- und Interessenslage der Lernenden berücksichtigen und damit die Bereitschaft der Schüler, sich mitzuteilen, nützen. Sie gehen nicht nur auf spezifisch landeskundliche Bereiche der Zielsprachekulturen ein, sondern sind auch von allgemeinem, fächerübergreifendem Interesse, wie z. B. die Themen Umweltprobleme, Reisen in andere Länder, zwischenmenschliche Beziehungen und Zukunftsprognosen. Schließlich beziehen die Themen interkulturelle Aspekte mit ein, wie z. B. Lebensweisen und -bedingungen in Ländern zusätzlich zu denen der Zielsprachekulturen, und fördern damit Offenheit in der Begegnung mit Menschen anderer Herkunft.
Interkulturelle Kommunikationskompetenz im Sinne von uneigennützigem Fremdverstehen fängt aber schon im Umgang mit dem nächsten Schüler und beim Verhältnis der Schüler untereinander an. Deshalb wurden neben der Möglichkeit zur lehrerzentrierten und Einzelarbeit sozialintegrative Beziehungsformen wie Partner- und Gruppenarbeit gewählt, die neben dem kognitiven vor allem das soziale Lernen fördern, gleichzeitig die Sprechzeit

der Lernenden beträchtlich erweitern und schließlich die Kommunikation wirklichen Wissens und realer Information mit wirklichen Kommunikationspartnern gewährleisten.

Die Begriffe „Schüler“ und „Lehrer“ werden im folgenden als neutrale Sammelbeziehungen verwendet, die jeweils beide Geschlechter umfassen.

1. Getting used to Britain

Visitors to other countries often find there are quite a few things they have to get used to. Look, for instance, at everything these visitors to Britain have to get used to:

Rajiv, from India, is trying to **get used to** *English food.*
He is trying to **get used to** *drinking tea* all day, too.

to get used to something
to get used to doing something } sich an etwas gewöhnen

1. Mineko usually has rice for breakfast in Japan. When she stayed in British hotels she couldn't eat the breakfasts of bacon and eggs.

She couldn't ________________________________ breakfast.

2. Pierre, from France, was surprised that British salads don't have dressings.

But he soon ________________________________ them and now he quite likes them.

3. Anna comes from Austria. She can't drink tea with milk, like they do in Britain.

She ________________________________ tea with milk. (drink)

4. Miriam is Nigerian. In Britain she always feels cold.

She is finding it hard to ________________ the British climate.

5. Carlos comes from Spain, where they drive on the right.

He has to ________________________

__________ on the left. And when he crosses the road

he has to ____________________ to the right first.

2. Two Germans in England

Dagmar and Andreas are on a school exchange to England from Germany.
There are quite a lot of things they have to get used to.

> *to be used to* something
> an etwas gewöhnt sein

- They **are not used to** going to school from nine to four every day.
- The English were surprised when they tried to shake hands with people all the time.

  They told them: "We're not ______________________ shaking hands."
- Dagmar kept forgetting to queue for buses.

  She ______________________________ for buses.
- It was a long time before they stopped saying "good appetite" before meals.

  They didn't know that the English ______________________________ .

3. Getting used to different places

Can you think of some things you found hard to get used to –
where you live now or in a country you once visited?

- In France it was hard to get used to speaking French all the time/ …
- I couldn't get used to/found it hard to get used to … in …
- When I first came here I wasn't used to …

What might visitors to Germany find it difficult to get used to?

- It might be difficult/hard to get used to the …/ … ing
- They/Someone from (Turkey) might have problems getting used to … /might not be used to …

4. Getting used to living alone

Diana has always lived at home with her parents.
Now she has got a job a hundred miles away, so she will have to get used to living alone.
Think of all the things she will have to get used to.

She'll have to get used to … /doing … eating alone

the/her own
shopping washing cleaning
ironing cooking
staying in alone …

5. I could never get used to it

Is there anything you think you could never get used to?

I could never get used to …

I don't think I could get used to …

I would find it very hard/difficult to get used to …

living in a cold climate tea with milk
living on my own
classical music being unemployed …

1. The way things used to be

Nobody knows you when you're down and out

Paul McNally was once a famous boxer, earning millions of pounds a year. In fact, he had so much money he didn't really know what to do with it. Most of it went on expensive clothes, big houses and fast cars. He never used to save any. Of course, he also paid people to do things for him – boring things like cooking and cleaning.

A few years ago, however, things started to go badly wrong. Paul loved going out with his friends in the evenings, dancing, drinking champagne and never going to bed before about three in the morning.

Eventually, this began to affect his training. He lost one fight after another and soon his sponsors dropped him. So, too, did most of his 'friends'. But Paul loved the good life so much, he just kept on spending.

About a year ago he was so much in debt that he lost all his possessions – the houses, the cars, everything. Finally, he had to give up professional boxing altogether.

Today Paul works as a boxing coach in a sports centre. His whole life-style has changed. Whereas he never used to do anything for himself, now he cooks his own meals, does his own washing and cleans his small flat himself. These days he never goes to either night clubs or parties and he can only afford cheap wine. He usually goes to bed early because he has to catch the seven o'clock bus to work. He no longer goes everywhere by taxi and is saving up to buy a car. Most evenings he stays in and reads or listens to music – things he never used to do. Paul's favourite song?

Paul **used to** drink champagne. He **never used to** do any cooking. He **didn't use to** save money.	**used to** – für Dauerzustände und Gewohnheiten in der Vergangenheit

Compare the way Paul used to live a few years ago with the way he lives now.

He *used to be* a famous boxer.

buy drink drive go
live pay see spend ... on
wear stay up

He *didn't use* to ...

clean cook do drink go live
listen read save stay in travel

Paul often thinks about the past. What does he say to himself?

I *never used to* stay in at night.
I *never used to* ...

2. How has your life changed?

Tell your partner how you've changed in the last few years. Talk about…

- places you used to go to
- where you used to go on holiday
- things you used to do in your free time
- what you used to look like
- the kind of music you used to like
- the kind of friends you used to have
- a favourite toy or pet that you used to have
- the kind of TV programmes you used to watch
- things you used to like or hate doing
- things you used to want
- things you used to dream about

I *used to* …

I *didn't use* to …

You: I used to save all my money, but I don't now.
Partner: Why not?
You: I'd rather buy things with it.
Partner: What kind of things?
You: …

You: I didn't use to like sports much.
Partner: And now?
You: …

Ask your classmates:

Did you **use** *to* … ?
What did you **use** *to* … ?
Where did …?

Did you use to collect anything?
What did you use to read?

Write down four or five things you can remember about your classmates, e.g.

Barbara used to …

Thomas used to …

3. Poems

Can you write a poem? It needn't rhyme.

I used to be rich and famous.
I never used to save money.
But now I only want a friend.

She used to work all day.
She didn't use to have holidays.
But now she wants to dream.

I used to
…
I never used to
…
But now …

He/She used to
…
He/She didn't use to
…
But now …

1. If things had been different

1. Last night Tony watched the late night film. That is why he went to bed late.

   If Tony had not watched the film he would have gone to bed earlier.

The next morning Tony got up late. That is why he did not catch the bus.

If Tony ______________ to bed earlier he *would not have got* up so late. (go)

If Tony ______________ up late he *would not have missed* the bus. (not get)

If Tony ______________ earlier he *could have caught* the bus. (get up)

2. Tony was late for work. That is why he lost his job.

______ Tony ______________ on time he probably *would not have lost* his job. (arrive)

______ Tony ______________ late for work he *might not have lost* his job. (not be)

3. Tony lost his job. Now he is washing up at McDonald's.

______ Tony ______________ he *would not be washing up* at McDonald's. (not lose)

Bedingung	Folgerung
If Tony *had gone* to bed earlier	he *would/could/might have caught* the bus.
If Tony *had* not *gone* to bed so late	he *would* not **be** wash*ing* up now.
If + past perfect	**would/could/might** (not) + **have** + *past participle* + **be -ing**
Nach *if* kein *would*	

↑ Hier kein Komma!

2. Sylvia's burglar

1. Sylvia went out and left the window open. That is why the burglar could get in.

   If Sylvia ______________________ the window open the burglar ______________ ____________ in. (not leave – not get)

2. The burglar dropped his car keys. That is why he did not get away very fast.

   ____ the burglar ______________________ his car keys he ______________________ faster. (not drop – get away)

3. The burglar did not get away fast enough. So the police caught him.

   ____ the burglar ______________________ faster the police ______________________ ____________ . (get away – not catch)

4. The police caught him. That is why he is in prison now.

   ____ the police ________________ him he ____________________ in prison now. (not catch – not be)

3. A life of crime

At eighteen Wayne Pickett is a car mechanic. He loves his job and is saving up to open his own garage one day. A few years ago, however, it was a very different story. In fact, if things had turned out differently he might have been in deep trouble by now.

1992	– left school at 14, couldn't get a job
	– started stealing cars
1993	– started taking drugs
	– broke into houses to pay for drugs

What might have been different?

If Wayne had stayed at school he might have found a job.

1. Today's phone messages

How good are you at taking phone messages?

1. An hour later you tell your sister:

   Dave rang. He said he ____________________ you in about ____________ .

2. An hour later you tell Carol:

   Alex rang. He said that they ____________________ ____________________ .

Please tell Brian I've bought six tickets for the football match next Saturday.

3. An hour later you tell Brian:

   Sue phoned. She said she ____________________ ____________________ .

Please tell John that I have to talk to him about something.

4. An hour later you tell John:

   Jean rang. She said she ____________________ ____________________ .

> Will man wörtliche Rede wiedergeben, muß man häufig eine Reihe von Veränderungen vornehmen. Zeitformen z.B. können, müssen aber dann **nicht verändert werden**, wenn die Aussage der wörtlichen Rede **noch in der Gegenwart zutrifft**.

Was hast du bei der Wiedergabe der Telefonnachrichten verändern müssen?

1. *I* → ____________________

2. ____________ 3. ____________ 4. ____________

2. Say or tell?

Which is correct – *said* or a form of *tell*?

1. Carol ________ they are meeting at seven.
2. Brian ________ me that he has bought six tickets.
3. Dave ________ that he will ring tonight.
4. Jean wants to ________ you something.

> Dave said he will ring.
> Dave *told me* he will ring.
> (*tell* + Person)

3. Phone messages – the next day

All these phone messages came yesterday. Can you pass them on correctly?

> Will you tell Carol that I'll phone her tonight, please.

1. **The next day** you tell Carol:

Alex rang last night. He asked me to ________ you that he ______________________________.

But you weren't in.

Die Aussage der direkten Rede trifft in der Gegenwart nicht mehr zu. Was muß deshalb verändert werden?

I'll → ________ , ________ → ____________

> Please tell Pete that I've bought tickets for the match this afternoon.

2. The next day you tell Pete:

Sue phoned yesterday to ____________ that she __________ __________ tickets for the match ____________ afternoon.

But you were out all day.

> Will you tell Maria that we're meeting here tonight, please. She knows where my flat is.

3. The next day you tell Maria:

Paul rang yesterday to ________ you that they ____________ ______________________________________.

But you weren't in.

> Please tell Pete that I'm listening to my new CDs. If he wants to he can come round.

4. The next day you tell Pete:

Ann phoned yesterday afternoon. She ________ she __________ ______________________________________ ______________________________________.

Was hast du bei der Wiedergabe der direkten Rede verändern müssen?

2. I've bought → ______________________________________

3. ______________________________________

4. ______________________________________

Say five times: Wood said he would carry wood through the wood.
Suzy said she would show Sue her shoe.

Beachte bei der Wiedergabe von direkter Rede:

"Please tell Brian **I've bought** tickets for the match **next Saturday.**"
Sue said she **has bought** tickets for the match **next Saturday.**

Trifft die Aussage der wörtlichen Rede **noch zu** (es ist noch nicht Samstag), können Zeitformen und Zeitbezüge **unverändert** bleiben.

"Please tell Pete **I've bought** tickets for this afternoon."
Paul said he **had bought** tickets for **yesterday** afternoon.

Trifft die Aussage der wörtlichen Rede **nicht mehr zu** (z. B. einen Tag danach), müssen Zeitformen und Zeitbezüge in die Vergangenheit **zurückverschoben** werden.

4. Is it really true?

Look at the way people's words are reported in these pairs of sentences.

1. Über welche Äußerung würdest du dich mehr freuen?
   a) Jane said you *are* very nice.
   b) Jane said you *were* very nice.

2. Bei welcher Äußerung hättest du eher den Verdacht auf Angeberei?
   a) Kevin told us that his father *has bought* a ranch.
   b) Kevin told us that his father *had bought* a ranch.

3. Bei welcher Äußerung würdest du vorsichtshalber am Freitag nachfragen?
   a) Diane told me she *is having* a party on Saturday.
   b) Diane told me she *was having* a party on Saturday.

4. Bei welcher Äußerung bist du eher sicher, dein Geld zurückzubekommen?
   a) Sue said she *would give* you your five pounds back next week.
   b) Sue said she *will give* you your five pounds back next week.

Trifft die Aussage der wörtlichen Rede zwar **noch zu**, die **Zeitformen** sind aber **verändert**, ist das oft ein Hinweis dafür, daß der Berichtende an der Aussage **zweifelt.**

Written on the grave of a hypochondriac:
See – I told you I was ill.

1. Problems with parents

Where are you going?
Who are you going with?

What are your friends like?
Where do they live?

What are you going to do when you leave school? How much will you earn?

Marion My mother always wants to know where I'm going and who I'm going with.	*Linda* My parents keep asking me about my friends – what they're like, where they live and things like that.	*Eric* My girlfriend's Dad is always asking me what I'm going to do when I leave school.

How would you answer these letters?
Can you suggest anything? (*try to/talk to/tell/say/explain/take … home meet/…*)

Marion/Linda/Eric could …

2. Too many questions

Die Elternfragen oben treffen im Moment ihrer Wiedergabe in den Leserbriefen noch zu. Welche sprachlichen Veränderungen fallen in den Leserbriefen auf? Was bleibt? Was kommt hinzu?

1. Where are you going? → Marion says to her friend: My mother always wants to know where I'm going.

Fragezeichen fällt weg, ______________________________

____

____

2. What are your friends like? → Linda says: My parents keep asking me what my friends are like …

____

____

____

3. Where do your friends live? → Linda tells her friend: My parents want to know where my friends live.

____

____

____

Wenn du Fragen mit Fragewörtern (**What? Where?** …) wiedergeben möchtest, und das in der Frage Ausgedrückte **noch zutrifft**, ergeben sich folgende Veränderungen:
– es **fallen weg**: Fragenzeichen, **do/does/did**
– es **bleiben**: Fragewort, Zeitformen
– es **kommt hinzu**: Einleitung (… **wants to know/asks/**…)
– es **ändern sich**: Personalpronomen, Wortstellung (wie in Aussagen)

3. Mary's problems

Last night Mary got home very late. Her parents asked her a lot of questions:

Where have you been?

Why are you so late?

Who were you with?

How did you get home?

Today Mary is telling her friend what happened last night.

Mary: My parents were really mad.
They asked me so many questions:

where ____________________

why ____________________ so late,

how ____________________ home,

who ____________________ and lots more.

Wenn das in der Frage Ausgedrückte **nicht mehr zutrifft** (z.B. am nächsten Tag), werden alle Zeitformen in die **Vergangenheit zurückverschoben.** Das *simple past* bleibt jedoch häufig unverändert.

4. My dream girl

Do you live round here?

Have you been here before?

Do you like dancing?

Do you prefer rock or pop music?

Have you been to the new disco in town?

Are you still at school?

Can you drive?

Are you here on your own or with your girlfriend?

Are you coming tomorrow night?

A 6 Indirekte Rede: Fragen

Last night Darren went to a disco. This morning he is telling his friend Ken about it.

Darren: I had a great time at the disco last night. I met a wonderful girl. She asked me to dance. I couldn't think of anything to say, but it didn't matter because she asked me lots of questions.

First she wanted to know **if I lived** near the disco.

Then she asked if ______________________________ before.

She wanted to know ______________________________ and whether ______________________________

______________ pop music.

whether –
eher bei Alternativfragen

She asked ____

She wanted to know ____

She also asked ____

And then she wanted to know ______________________________ on my own or with my girlfriend.

And then – you'll never believe it – she asked me ______________________________

Bei der **Wiedergabe von Fragen ohne Fragewort** geschieht folgendes:

- **do/does/did fallen weg**
- Einleitung (**She asked/wanted to know**) und **if/whether kommen hinzu**
- **Zeitbezüge ändern sich**, wenn die Frage nicht mehr zutrifft
- **Pronomen ändern sich**
- Wörter wie **here** und **there** kann man nur aus der Situation der direkten Rede heraus verstehen, deshalb müssen sie in der Wiedergabe näher erläutert werden.

Say five times:
Our Joe wants to know if your Joe will lend our Joe his banjo.

→ exotic holiday (e.g. Barbados, Tobago → West Indies or Bali
→ preparing an ~

→ Dos / Don'ts

Dos and don'ts

Miriam and her friends want to go on an exotic holiday this summer, perhaps to Africa or India. She has brought an information leaflet back from the travel agent's.

Going to a foreign country?

Do

- get information about passports, visas and health insurance
- find out how much money you are allowed to take into the country
- carry valuables on your person
- take any medicines you need with you
- learn some basic language
- buy guides and maps before you go
- check the opening times of shops, banks, museums etc.
- tell the post office you are going away

Don't

- take a lot of cash
- take valuables with you (e.g. jewelry)
- carry a lot of cash round with you
- leave your valuables in the hotel room
- take too much luggage
- eat anything that is not cooked, washed in clean water or peeled
- expect everything to be like it is at home
- ignore local customs and traditions
- forget that you are a guest in someone else's country

Read this information carefully and try to remember it.
Now cover it up.
How much information can you give your classmates about "exotic" holidays?

They *tell/ask/advise you to* … They *tell/ask/advise/warn you not to* …

So geben wir Ratschläge und Aufforderungen wieder:

They **advise**	**you**	**to get** information about passports.
They **ask**	**people**	**not to take** a lot of cash.
tell/ask/advise +	Person +	*(not) to* + Infinitiv

They suggest — should —

1. My dream job

What would you like to be when you leave school? Why?
What is your dream job? What do you think you will do?

Play this game: A: I work outside. I don't see many people. What's my job?
B: Are you a/an …?

Jobs: *a* gardener
an architect

work indoors/
with a lot of people
at night/
in an office
visit people
sell/repair things
use languages
write a lot
be famous

Ask your partner: What would you rather be – a teacher or a truck driver?

– a/an … or a/an …?

2. A quiz

Who were these people?

1. Cleopatra	Muslim
2. Homer	Communist
3. Raphael	politician
4. Mohammed	Egyptian
5. St. Nicholas	Nobel prizewinner
6. Rosa Luxemburg	Emperor
7. Marie Curie	Italian
8. Indira Gandhi	Catholic
9. Barbarossa	Greek

a/an für Zugehörigkeit zu:
- einem Beruf
- einer Nationalität, Konfession, Partei
- Gruppen mit besonderen Eigenschaften (Nobelpreisträger, Vegetarier usw.)

1. Cleopatra was a/an …
2. Homer was …

3. How often?

How often do you do these things? Ask your partner.

How often do you
- wash your hands?
- brush your teeth?
- do sports?
- go swimming?
- go dancing?
- go to the cinema?
- buy clothes?
- listen to or watch the news?
- read a magazine?
- read a newspaper?

never

several times
an hour

once, twice,
three times
a day/month

4. British measurements

How much is:

1. a mile?
   a) about half a kilometre
   b) a bit more than 1 1/2 kilometres

2. a yard?
   a) just under a metre
   b) about half a metre

3. 100 miles an hour?
   a) about 130 kilometres an hour
   b) about 160 kilometres an hour

4. a pint?
   a) about a quarter of a litre
   b) about half a litre

5. a pound (weight)?
   a) about half a kilogram
   b) about 1 1/2 kilos

a/an for *measuring* things:
- half *a* mile
- a quarter of *a* litre
- forty pence *a* pound

1. Advertisements and notices

Look at this poster.
How would you translate the underlined words into German?

1.

Was fällt dir auf? Was ist im Deutschen anders?
Suche Beispiele aus diesen Anzeigen und Schilderaufschriften für die folgenden Regeln.

2.

3.

4.

5.

6.

7.

8.

9.

Im Englischen **kein the** vor:

1. **Monaten, Tagen, Mahlzeiten**, wenn sie **in verallgemeinernder Bedeutung** gebraucht werden: ____________________
2. Wörtern wie *school, hospital,* wenn wir an die **Institutionen** und nicht an bestimmte Gebäude denken: ____________________
3. den meisten **Eigennamen**, z.B. von Menschen, Straßen, Brücken, Plätzen, Gebäuden (Ausnahmen: *the* USA, *the* Eiffel Tower): ____________________
4. abstrakten Begriffen: ____________________
5. einigen anderen Ausdrücken: ____________________

2. Life

In English we use *the* when we mean a specific day, month, meal, or place, for example:

the [ðə] vor Konsonanten: **the cat, the Germans**
[ðɪ] vor Vokalen: **the apple, the English**

but

Finish each pair of sentences with the words on the right. Decide when to use *the*.

1. a) I only have a sandwich for ____________ .
   b) Do you remember ____________ we had together last year?
2. a) My brother goes to ____________ every Sunday.
   b) Where is ____________ that your brother goes to?
3. a) I am leaving ____________ next year.
   b) ____________ I go to is great.
4. a) Are you looking forward to going to ____________ ?
   b) Yes. ____________ I'll be doing is very interesting.
5. a) ____________ where I was born is in the North.
   b) Let's go to ____________ and look round the shops.

lunch
church
school
work
town

3. Finding out about your partner

Ask your partner all these questions. Then your partner asks you.

1. What time do you get up in …? (morning)
2. What time do you go to … in …? (bed – week)
3. What time do you go to … at …? (bed – weekend)
4. What do you usually do in …? (afternoon)
5. How often do you go to …? (cinema).
   How many times a month?
6. Do you listen to … often? (radio)
7. Do you play … or …? (piano – guitar)

in the { morning / evening / week
at the weekend

go to *the* cinema, theatre
listen to *the* radio
play *the* piano, guitar

1. Bored with life

Alex works for a teenage magazine. He answers readers' letters.
This is one of the letters that he received a few months ago.

Dear Alex

I'm so bored with life. Nothing ever changes. I've been doing the same things day after day, week after week for years now. I want to do something different, but I don't know what.
I've been working in the same office since I left school four years ago – doing the same job, talking to the same people, listening to the same old stories, having lunch in the same canteen every single day. The weekends aren't much better either.
On Saturday nights I always go to the same disco with some old school friends. We've been going there since we left school.
I'm even bored with my holidays. I've been going to the same place for years.
I'm fed up with the way I look, too. My hair always looks the same, probably because I've been going to the same hairdresser since I was a child. And I don't like my clothes any more, either. I've been wearing the same style for years.
Can you make any suggestions?

Laura

Before Alex can make any suggestions he needs to write down everything that Laura is bored with in her life. What does he write?

For years now Laura has been doing the same things day after day.

1. She ______________________ in the same office since she left school.
2. She ______________________ the same job.
3. ____ the same people.
4. ____ stories.
5. ____ canteen.
6. ____ the same kind of things at weekends.
7. _______________________________________ every Saturday night ________ she left school.
8. _______________________________________ for her holidays ________ years.
9. ________________________________ the same ____________________ she was a child.
10. _____________________________________ style of clothes ________ years.

What suggestions would you make?

Laura **has been doing** the same things for years.	Mit dem **present perfect continuous** betonen wir die bisherige **Dauer** eines Geschehens.

Which tense shows this in German? Find out by translating the sentence in the box.

2. A new life

Alex answered Laura's letter.
Last week she sent him another letter and photo.

Dear Alex

This is the new me. I've changed my job. That meant moving to a different town, but I love it here. I've made some new friends and I've started playing table-tennis. I've also joined a chess club. Thanks again for your help.

Laura

What has Laura done?
She has changed …

I've been doing the same thing for years. Wenn wir betonen wollen, **wie lange** etwas schon **andauert**, gebrauchen wir das …	**I've changed** my job. Wenn wir uns eher für das **Ergebnis** interessieren, verwenden wir das …

3. What about you?

Talk about what you do in your spare time.

I play volleyball/collect stamps/…

How long have you been playing/collecting them/…

For/Since …

4. Can you tell these jokes?

Doctor: You should stop taking those sleeping pills. You'll get used to them.
Patient: No, I won't. I … them for fifteen years. (take)

Dentist: Stop screaming. I haven't started yet.
Girl: I know. But you … on my foot for the last five minutes. (stand)

1. Holidays

All these people are going on holiday next week.
They're imagining what they will be doing next week.

This time next week I **won't be** work**ing** in this office. I'**ll be** climb**ing** Snowdon.

> Wenn wir uns **vorstellen**, was wir zu einem bestimmten Zeitpunkt in der Zukunft gerade tun bzw. nicht tun, gebrauchen wir das **future continuous**.
>
> This time next week I **won't be** work**ing** in this office.
> I'**ll be** climb**ing** Snowdon.

What will all these people be doing this time next week? What won't they be doing?

1. (Liz – sell clothes – lie on the beach)

2. (Mike and Alison – do homework – hike)

3. (Jenny and Christine – do people's hair – sail)

4. (Paul – clean windows – sightsee)

5. (Ralph and Kevin – drive taxis – fish)

6. (Tracy – repair computers – pony trek)

7. (Derek – work in a bank – tour, Wales)

8. (Charlie – sell cars – live on a boat)

2. Plan your own holiday in Britain

Which of these holidays would you like best?

Great British Holidays

Come to the UK for a holiday.
There are lots of great ideas to choose from:

- *tour* different parts of the country
- *go sightseeing*
- *walk* on the cliffs in Devon
- *visit* old castles and museums
- *go fishing* in Scotland
- *try pony trekking* in Northern Ireland
- *go bird watching* in Cornwall
- *go cycling* in Yorkshire
- *live on a house boat* on the Norfolk Broads
- *go sailing* round the Isle of Wight
- *go hiking* in the Lake District
- *or just lie on a beach and relax*

Ask someone in your class:

- Are you doing anything next week?
  Perhaps we could go somewhere?
- Sorry. This time next week I'll be ...ing

sightseeing in ...
visiting ...
touring Northern Ireland
fishing in the Thames
cycling in Scotland

1. Simon's week

Look at what Simon is doing next week.

Write down Simon's fixed plans for next week in the order of the weekdays.

1. **Next Monday** Simon **is babysitting** for the Browns at half past seven.
2. On Tuesday ______
3. ______
4. ______
5. ______
6. ______
7. ______
8. ______

Simon **is** baby**sitting next Monday** – **present continuous** für **feste Vereinbarungen** in der **Zukunft**

2. Jokes

Can you tell these jokes?

1. Are you using your bike this afternoon?
2. Footballer: I know how we can improve the team.
3. We're sending our little Sammy to a holiday camp this summer.
4. We're having my mother for Christmas dinner.

a) – Does he need a holiday?
 – No. We do.

b) – Yes.
 – Good. Then I can use your car.

c) Are you? We're having turkey.

d) Manager: Good. When are you leaving?

3. Are you doing anything tonight?

Fill in this diary for next week.

13 Mon ____________	17 Fri ____________
____________	____________
____________	____________
14 Tues ____________	18 Sat ____________
____________	____________
____________	____________
15 Wed ____________	19 Sun ____________
____________	____________
____________	____________
16 Thurs ____________	
____________	
____________	

Find a time when you can go and see your partner.

You: Can I come and see you sometime?
Partner: Yes, of course. When?
You: Are you doing anything on (Wednesday afternoon)?
Partner: Sorry, I'm …/No, (Wednesday)'s fine. What time?
You: Then what about …?/…

4. What are you doing next week?

Ask your partner:

What are you doing (after school today/this …/tomorrow night/at the weekend/next week)?

Write down what you have found out about your partner:

… is … ing … on/next …
Next/On … he/she is … -ing …

1. A tour of London

Yvonne is a tourist guide. She is telling a group of German pupils about her firm's tours of London.

"I'll just give you a general idea of the tour. We can fill in the details later. We leave Ostend on Saturday afternoon on the half past two ferry. Four and a half hours later we arrive at Ramsgate.
The next morning at ten we leave for London by coach. The journey takes about two hours. When we get to London we first check in at the hotel. That takes about an hour. Then we have lunch. We start our three hour bus tour of London an hour later.
When that's over we go on an hour's walking tour of London's theatre district. This tour finishes outside your hotel. You then have an hour before we set off for the theatre. The play starts at eight and goes on for two and a half hours.
The next morning at ten we have a boat trip. That takes two hours. Then, after an hour's break for lunch, we go on a three hour walking tour of the new dockland area. After that we take you back to your hotel for a rest."

Would you like to go on this tour? Can you fill in the details?

Sat. leave Ostend	14.30
arrive Ramsgate	______
______	______
______	______
______	______
______	______
______	______
______	______
______	______
______	______
______	______
______	______
______	______
______	______

We **leave** Ostend at 14.30. When **does** the play **start**?	**Simple present** für die **Zukunft**, wenn etwas **programm**- oder **fahrplanmäßig** abläuft.

2. Checking the details

Imagine you are going on this tour.
Your partner is the tourist guide.
Check the details. Find out when you:

- leave Ostend (When do we …?)
- arrive at Ramsgate?
- leave Ramsgate?

Now you are the tourist guide and your partner needs information.
Your partner:

- arrive in London?
- check in at the hotel?
- have lunch?

Now it's your turn again to ask for information:

- When … bus tour of London …? (start)
- When … the bus tour over? (be)
- When … the walking tour of the theatre district? (be)
- What time … this walking tour …? (finish)
- How … we … back to the hotel? (get)
- What time … we … for the theatre? (set off)
- When … the play …? (start)
- How long … the play … for? (go on)

Your partner's turn to ask for information:

- When … the boat trip? (be)
- Which river … we … on? (go)
- How long … the boat trip …? (take)
- What … we … after the boat trip? (do)
- How long … we … for lunch? (have)
- And then what … we …? (do)
- What time … we … back to the hotel? (get)

"I've got that job. You start on Monday."

1. Finding your way around London

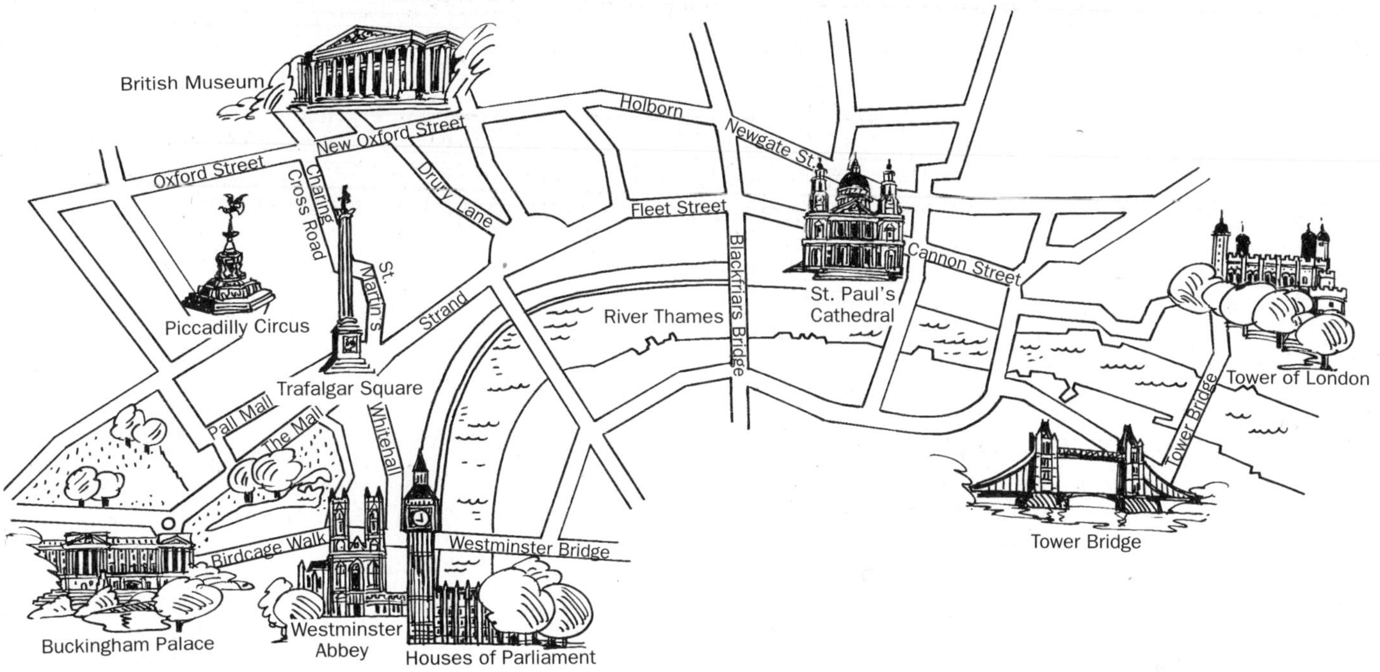

Could you find your way around London? Let's see. You are at Trafalgar Square. Someone asks you:

1. Could you tell me the way to the British Museum, please?

You: Of course. Go down … *As soon as you come* to a crossroads … The British Museum is just … the road.

2. Could you tell me the way to Buckingham Palace, please?

You: Oh, yes. Just go down … *until you come* to a big building. That's it.

3. Could you tell me the way to the river, please?

You: Of course. Go down … and *when you get* to a T-junction … and … on.

As soon as you come to a crossroads turn right.
Go down the road **until you come** to a big building.
When you get to a crossroads turn left.

Beziehen sich **as soon as, until, when** auf die **Zukunft**, gebraucht man das **simple present (nicht will)**.

2. Giving directions

1. You are at Westminster Abbey. Ask your partner for directions to Blackfriars Bridge.

You: Could you …?
Your partner: Turn … As soon as you … (be) on the other side of the river turn …
Go straight on until you … (come) to a big … Keep going straight on.
When you … (get) to the next … turn …

2. Your partner asks you for directions to St Paul's.

   You: Go down … As soon as you … to Trafalgar Square turn … Go on until … a big crossroads. Go … When you … to the next … go … St Paul's … on your left.

3. You are at the Tower of London. Ask your partner for directions to Westminster Abbey.

   Your partner: Go … down … Street. When … a big crossroads go straight on. Don't go down to the river. Go on until you … another … Again, go … Keep going until … Trafalgar Square. When … Trafalgar Square turn … down … until … a T-junction. Westminster Abbey … across …

4. Your partner asks you for directions to Buckingham Palace.

   You: Go … down … Street until … a big crossroads. Turn … When … to the river cross … Bridge. As soon as you … the other side of the river turn … When … a big crossroads go … Keep going until … the next big … Then … onto … Bridge. Go … until … another big … Go … on until … the end of … Walk. Buckingham Palace … in front of you.

3. Moving to London

Pauline has got a job in London. So she is going to live there.

Some friends are saying goodbye at the station.

as soon as you arrive when I've booked until I've found	**as soon as, when, until** **+ simple present/present perfect für die Zukunft** **(nicht will arrive/will have booked usw.).**

What else do Pauline and her friends say?

	Pauline:
Steve: Will you write to me?	Of course. But not until I … a permanent address. (got)
Jenny: I'll come and stay with you when I … on holiday. (be)	Great. I'll write as soon as I … a flat. (find)
Derek: I can't come to see you until I … some money. (save)	All right. Let me know when you … enough. (get)
Ann: I think I'd like to live in London, too.	We'll talk about it when you … to see me. (come)
Sue: I'm coming to London sometime next month.	Great. Write to me as soon as you … the date. (know)

1. The year 2100

Experts cannot agree what the world will look like by the year 2100.
Read the first sentence to your partner and find out what he or she thinks.
Then your partner reads the next sentence to you.

By the year 2100

1. Most people in Europe will have bought solar cars.
2. The atmosphere will not have improved.
3. Trains, trams and buses will mostly have replaced cars.
4. Most people will have moved out of the cities.
5. Many types of animals, insects and plants will have gone.
6. Some cultures and languages will have disappeared.
7. The world's forests will not have died.
8. There will not have been a catastrophic nuclear accident.
9. We will not have solved the rubbish problem.
10. We will have used up all the world's oil. The sun, wind and water will be used for energy.
11. The USA will have had a black president.
12. More women will have become politicians.
13. The world's population will not have changed much.
14. Poverty will not have increased.
15. Doctors will not have found a cure for aids.
16. We will not have solved the problem of unemployment.
17. Letters will have disappeared. People will use fax machines and E-mail instead.
18. Telephone boxes will have disappeared. Most people will use a mobile phone.
19. Schools will not have changed much.
20. Cash will have disappeared. Everything will be paid for by credit cards.
21. Sportspeople will have broken all today's records.

will (not) have + past participle **(won't = will not)**	Um auszudrücken, daß etwas zu einem bestimmten Zeitpunkt in der Zukunft **passiert sein wird** bzw. **nicht passiert sein wird.**

With a partner or in a group write down some things that you think will or won't have happened by the year 2100.

2. The world's population

Can you interpret this graph?
In 1950 the world's population was about 2.5 billion.

In … it was about …
Scientists say that by 2025 it … and by … it …
(increase – grow to)

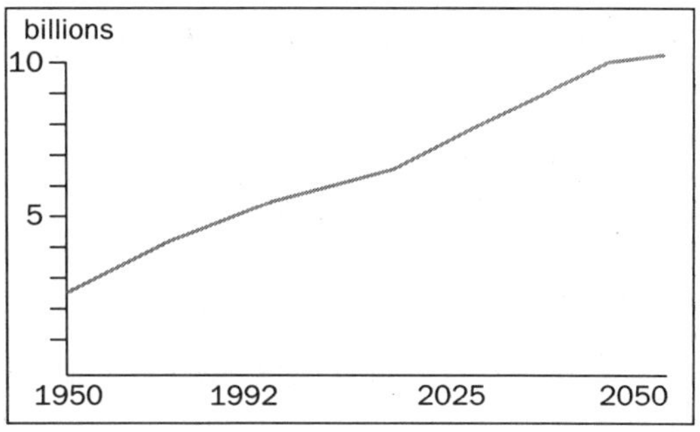

1. Holidays

Come to Sunnydale Camp in Devon – we have lots of things for you to do

Lots of things for all the family to enjoy.

Clean beaches for you to swim or just lie on the sand.

If you are the active type there are courses for you to learn tennis and sailing. There is also lovely countryside for you to go for walks or bike rides.

Bring your tent or stay in one of our bungalows.
All bungalows have kitchens for you to cook your own meals.

There are lots of things **for you to do**.
The bungalows have kitchens **for you to cook** your own meals.

Die Struktur **for** + Objekt + **to**-Infinitiv wird oft verwendet, um auszudrücken, welchen Zweck oder welche Möglichkeiten eine Sache für jemanden hat (häufig nach **there is** und **have**).

Would you be able to work for an advertising agency? Make some posters to advertise these places: Write sentences like this: (There are/We have) clean beaches for you/(young) people/children to …

1. **Sunnylands holiday camp**

Beautiful beaches for you to swim or just relax.
A playground – children
A disco – all the latest dances
A kiosk – your favourite newspapers and magazines
Courses – sailing and surfing
Organised games
A campsite – your tent
Lots of interesting places
Boats

buy
enjoy themselves
get to know people
hire
learn
put up
visit

2. **Good Fun holiday village**

Lovely beaches
Bikes
A games room – table-tennis
A cinema – your favourite films
A library – books
A café – a quick snack
A laundrette

borrow
do your washing
have
hire
play
see

1. What job do I do?

Who said this about their jobs? Quite often there is more than one answer.

1. Some classes are wonderful to work with, others are not.
2. It's marvellous to see so many different countries.
3. It's helpful to speak different languages.
4. Some customers are very difficult to please.
5. It's important to look good all the time.
6. Planes are not difficult things to fly.
7. It's exciting to know you're the only person up there.
8. It's wonderful to be able to help people.
9. It's fun to make people look better.
10. Working at night is hard to get used to.
11. It's important to like repairing things.
12. It's nice to work with beautiful materials.
13. Animals are great to work with.
14. It's great to work outdoors.
15. It's wonderful to create something.
16. It's exciting to create new combinations.
17. The physical work was hard to get used to at first.
18. Sometimes it's hard to tell people they can't have more money.
19. The streets are quite difficult to learn.
20. It's important to have computer skills in my job.

shop assistant
waiter
hairdresser
builder
teacher
cook
air hostess
model
tourist guide
night watchman
gardener
pilot
hotel manager
fashion designer
hotel manager
vet
farmer
bank manager
taxi driver
secretary
astronaut
doctor
nurse

It's helpful to speak different languages. Animals **are great to work with.**	Wenn wir etwas **werten** wollen, sagen wir: **It/Nomen + be + Adjektiv + to-Infinitiv**

2. What do I do?

Think of a job and describe it like this:

In my job it's important to like/be …

Can the others guess what you do?

independent/creative/friendly/
good-looking/…

making things with your hands
organising/repairing things
being outdoors
doing physical work
working on problems/
with figures/machines
being with/helping people

3. What jobs do they do?

1. I. P. Lot.
2. Tod Cor
3. H. O. Grapthrope
4. Dan Greer
5. Neil Campo
6. Rolf E. Bloat
7. Mona P. Swot

Can you make up some more like this?

1. A questionnaire

What sort of person are you?
Answers: Yes, often – sometimes – not always – not very often – no, never – It depends – …

1. What do you want to do in your life? ______
2. What would you learn to do, if you could? ______
3. When you go somewhere new do you mostly expect to enjoy yourself? ______
4. Do you usually find it easy to decide to do things? ______
5. Do you often plan to do something, then forget to do it? ______
6. Do you often forget to do things? ______
7. Do you often promise to do things and then forget about them? ______
8. Do you usually agree to do what others want? ______
9. How often do you offer to help other people? ______
10. Do you often refuse to help others? ______
11. Do you mostly expect to get what you want? ______

What do you **want to do**? How often do you **offer to help**?	**to + Infinitiv** nach: **agree, decide, expect, forget, learn, offer, plan, promise, refuse, want, would**

2. What I want in life

Write down a few things about yourself:

I want to …
I'd like to learn to …
I've decided to …

3. A joke

Can you tell this joke?

Two business partners ______ on holiday together. (plan/go)

As they get on the plane one says, "I think I ______ the office safe." (forget/close)

The other answers, "That's all right. We're both here."

1. Running away from home

Last night two happy parents collected their daughter, Mary, from a London police station, two hundred miles from where they live.
A woman had met Mary on the train and had bought her a meal. Mary told the woman that she had run away from home.

At home Mary's parents wanted to know why she had run away. What did Mary tell them?

Mary's father: Can't you wear different clothes?

Her mother: Why don't you change your hairstyle?

Mary: Everybody keeps telling me what to do. Sometimes I just don't know what to do any more.

Dad **wants me to** wear different clothes.

"Mum tells ____"

Mother: Don't go out so often at night.

Mary: "Mum ____________________ **not to** ______________________________" (tell)

Father: Don't play your music so loud. — "Dad ..." (ask)

want/tell someone (not) to do something

Father: Don't leave school without good qualifications. — "He ..." (warn)

Grandmother: Why don't you come to see me more often?

"Grandma ... go and see ..." (ask)

Parents: No, you can't go on holiday with your friends.

"You ..." (allow)

Teachers: You should go to college. — "One teacher ..." (expect)

Teachers: Don't go to college. Get a job. — "Another teacher doesn't ... , but to get ..." (want)

Mother:

You should be a teacher.

"Mum …" (want)

Sister:

Don't get a job yet. Go and see the world first.

"Julie … job yet, but to … (tell)

Boyfriend:

Don't go away from home.

"Mike …" (want)

Uncle:

Don't wait too long before you decide.

"Uncle …" (advise)

Um Wunsch, Aufforderung, Verbot, Rat oder Warnung auszudrücken:

Mum **wants me to** be a teacher.	**want**	+ Objekt + **(not) to** Infinitiv	
Mike **doesn't want me to** go away.	**allow**		
They **don't allow me to** go on	**tell**	**me**	**to go away**
holiday with friends.	**ask**	**him**	**not to go away.**
Julie **tells me not to** get a job yet.	**expect**	**her**	
	warn	**us**	
	advise	**them**	

What do you think Mary and the others should do to improve the situation?

2. Other people

What would you like other people to do?
What do you want them to stop doing?
What don't you want them to do?

I want	my friend	
I'd like	my …	to
I don't want	people	
	…	

go to … with me
go out with me
stop talking about …
stop telling/asking me to …
stop calling me …
listen to me more

What do you hate?

I hate it when people
want/ask/tell/expect me (not) to …

I hate it when people
don't want/allow me to …

use my things   read my letters
laugh at my friends   check my homework
come into my room without asking …

1. Brothers and sisters

Sometimes people in the same family are very different, aren't they?
Look at these brothers and sisters.

Brian: I enjoy doing quiet things. For example, I like reading and painting. I don't mind being alone. I also like making things. I'd like to have more time for that, really. I'm not a very active person, so I avoid doing energetic things, like sports.

Pam: I'm very energetic. For example, I like to get up early, so I can pack as much as possible into every day. I prefer moving around to staying in the same place all the time. I like being with other people and I love going out with friends in the evenings and at weekends.

Mary:
Sometimes I want to be with other people, but sometimes I prefer to be on my own. It depends how I feel. I hate following routines. I'd hate to plan everything all the time. I couldn't stand doing the same things every day.

Which person is like you? Why?

…, because he/she enjoys/doesn't like/…

Which person would you prefer as your friend? Why?

…, because he/she doesn't mind/loves/can't stand …

2. I just love doing grammar

Make two lists like this. Find examples from the three descriptions.

Verbs followed by the -ing form	**Verbs followed by the infinitive**
I **enjoy doing** quiet things … (Brian)	**I'd like to have** more time … (Brian)
…	…

Look at your two lists and complete these rules:

1. These verbs can be followed by the *-ing* form or the infinitive …

Nach **would + like/love/hate/ prefer** steht der **to**-Infinitiv

2. Zum Ausdruck **allgemeiner** Vorlieben oder Abneigungen folgt auf *love, hate, like* und *prefer* die *-ing* Form, z.B.: …

Sometimes I **prefer to be** on my own
I **like to get** up early.

Der **Infinitiv** wird vorwiegend zum Ausdruck **konkreter Handlungen** verwendet. **Like + to:** das bin ich gewohnt, das finde ich gut/richtig.

What sort of person are you? Write on a piece of paper, but don't put your name on it:

I enjoy/don't like, mind/avoid/... **-ing**
I'**d** like/hate **to** ...

3. Some jokes

Patient: Doctor, people keep ignoring me.
Doctor: Next, please.

– How can I stop my dog barking in the front garden?
– Put him in the back garden.

keep
stop } + **-ing**

Tell these jokes by putting in the correct forms of the verbs.

1. Patient: Doctor, doctor, I ... I'm invisible. (keep – think)
   Doctor: Who said that?

2. Why did the taxi driver give up his job?
   Because people ... behind his back. (keep – talk)

3. Dentist: Please ..., I haven't started yet. (stop – shout)
   Boy: I know. But you're standing on my foot.

4. – I ... it's Monday. (keep – think)
   – But it is Monday.
   – I know. That's why I ... it's Monday. (keep – think)

5. Patient: Doctor, doctor, I ... my memory. (keep – lose)
   Doctor: When did that start?
   Patient: When did what start?

6. – Doctor, doctor, I ... I'm a kangaroo. (keep – think)
   – Rubbish! Hop off and take these pills. And be careful of your tail when you shut the door.

7. Teacher: Johnny, your homework is much better these days.
   Johnny: That's because my father has ... me. (stop – help)

8. Mother: So you didn't pass the history exam?
   Susan: No, they ... me about things that happened before I was born. (keep – ask)

1. Did you remember to do it?

You promised to do these things for your partner:

- go to the bank
- phone the hairdresser
- collect his/her jacket from the cleaner's
- get him/her an new exercise book
- buy a CD
- ask about train times
- buy some eggs

Your partner promised to do these things for you:

- post letter
- buy stamps
- buy a battery
- get some more dog food
- buy my magazine
- take my library books back
- get my watch repaired

You both forgot three things. Tick (✓) the things you remembered, but don't show your partner. Now find out what your partner remembered to do:

A: Did you remember to post my letter? – B: Yes, I did / Sorry, I forgot.
B: Did you remember to go to the bank? – A: …

What did you both forget to do?

I forgot to … My partner forgot to …

2. I always forget it

Is there anything that you always forget to do? Or someone you know?

I/My (father) always forget(s) to …
I/My … can never remember to …

Ask your partner:

You: How do you remember names/English words/numbers/to do …/…?
Partner: By …/… And you?

Write down some things you must remember to do in the next few days.

I must remember to/mustn't forget to …

3. I remember doing it

Write down some things you remember doing when you were younger.
Write down some things you will never forget doing.

I remember … ing (…)
I will never forget … ing (…)

learning to	meeting
going to	falling
seeing	breaking

remember / **forget** } **to**		**remember** / **forget** } **-ing**
Für etwas, was … ist.	→ Handlung ←	Für etwas, was … ist.

4. Stop

Describe these pictures by using either *stop + infinitive* or *stop + -ing.*

1.

Carol stopped … some chocolate. *(eat)*

Sue stopped … chocolate ages ago.

stop to do something
aufhören, um etwas zu tun

stop doing something
aufhören, etwas zu tun

2.

Brian … two years ago. *(smoke)*

Eric … smoke a cigarette.

3.

Lynne … coke a few months ago. *(buy)*

Diane … some coke.

5. Try

How can you help these people? Make suggestions by using *try to* or *try -ing.*

try doing something
etwas ausprobieren

try to do something
sich bemühen, etwas zu tun

1. I'm so tired. – Try … (sleep)
2. I can't sleep. – Try … a boring book. (read)
3. My boyfriend's always late. – … late yourself. (be)
4. My parents won't let me stay out overnight. – … their feelings. (understand)
5. I'm trying to learn Spanish. – Have you tried … cassettes? (use)
6. I'm nervous about the exam. – You'll be alright. Just … (relax)

1. Aren't these Earth people funny?

Some Martians went to have a look at the Earth.
When they got back home they told everyone what they had seen there.

We **watched some girls talking** inside a small box. Then we **saw someone press** a knob and suddenly the girls were gone.

1. We watched some people go into a big building and take things off shelves. Then we saw them put the things into bags and go out again.
2. We heard machines driving around all night. We couldn't sleep.
3. We saw people press buttons. Then it went dark and we saw them lie down on long things.
4. We heard things singing very early one morning. Then we saw them fly over our heads.
5. We felt something warming our faces all the time. Once we felt something wet falling on us. Then we saw people stop to put round things up over their heads.
6. We saw people putting things into their mouths with metal instruments.
7. We watched a woman put a roll of paper into her mouth. Then we saw her set fire to it!
8. We heard a small box ring. Then we saw someone go and talk into it.
9. We watched a man put something white into a red box on the wall.
10. We smelled something burning, so we went to have a look. We watched a big truck put lots of stuff on the ground. It looked awful.
11. We saw hundreds of people sitting in a big box with something green in the middle. We saw some men running with a round thing. We heard everybody shouting, but we couldn't understand them. Then we heard them shout 'goal'.
12. We sat on something green. It was nice and soft. But suddenly we felt something bite us.
13. We saw people wearing things like thin hats. But then we heard music coming out of them.
14. We heard music coming out of two big boxes.
15. We saw people sliding down hills on something white.
16. We saw a boy and girl put their lips together. How unhygienic!
17. We watched two men on a platform hitting each other. How stupid.

We **watched some girls talking** inside a small box. We **saw someone press** a knob.	Um Sinneswahrnehmungen zu beschreiben, verwenden wir: **see/hear** usw. + Objekt + { **-ing** Form / Infinitiv ohne **to**

Schau dir die Aussagen der Marsmenschen an.
Kannst Du erklären, wann die *-ing* Form verwendet wird und wann der Infinitiv?

2. What did the Martians see?

Can you explain what the Martians saw? Start with

They saw/watched/heard/felt/smelled …

These words will help you: *answer (phone), birds, box, eat, football match, go to bed, insects, kiss, loudspeakers, personal stereos, phone, post, rain, rubbish, shopping, ski, smoke, sun, umbrellas.*

Example:

We watched some girls talking inside a small box. Then we saw someone press a knob and suddenly the girls were gone.

They *saw someone watching* television.

1. They saw people go … ing.
2. They heard cars … all night.
3. They …

3. Through Martian eyes

Imagine you are a Martian. Tell your friends about your visit to Earth.

I saw/watched/heard …

4. A limerick

Mrs Wright had a fright*
In the middle of the night.
She saw a ghost eating toast
Half-way up a lamp-post.

* to have a fright – einen Schrecken bekommen

Can you think of some funny things like this?

I saw a dog playing the guitar …
I heard a cat bark …

5. Some jokes

Can you tell these jokes?

Teacher: I hope I didn't … at Andy's test paper, Mike? (see/look)
Mike: I hope you didn't, too.

Mary: I hear your boyfriend's a bad driver.
Jean: Yes. Even the lights go white when they … (see/come)

1. Who is it?

All these people are at an airport. Can you give them their names? Don't let your partner see what you are writing.
John is reading a newspaper. Tracy and Gina are eating crisps. Alison is having a cup of tea. Frank is sitting next to Sandra. Gina is carrying an umbrella.

Ask your partner:

You:	Who's the man wearing the raincoat?
Your partner:	Who's the … … ing tea?
You:	… wearing the anorak?
	sitting on the left of …?
	carrying …?
	other girl/eat …?

Look at this sentence. What's the different?

Who's the **man wearing** the raincoat?
Instead of the **man wearing** we could say the …

2. Would you know what to do?

Look at all the signs at the airport. Do you know what they all mean?

People who ________ in Europe have to ________________

____

There ________ board which ________ information ________

____

> Relative clauses with **who/which/that** can often be shortened by using **-ing** forms, especially after *There is/are*:
>
> Who's the **man wearing** the raincoat?
> **People living** in Europe …
> There is a **board giving** information …

Use short sentences with -ing forms to explain these notices:

Those ____

____ (travel)

People ________________ for a plane ________________

____ (wait)

There are taxis ________________ at ________________

____ (wait)

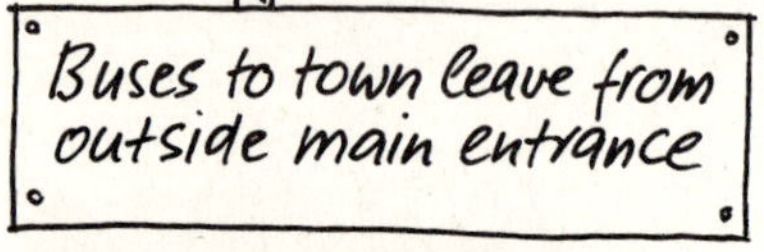

There ________________ to town ________________ from

____ (leave)

There ________________________ by ________

____ (stand)

Anyone ________________________ for the first time can ________________________ (visit)

Anyone ____

________________________ hotel information board (need)

People ____

____ (stay)

1. How much do you know about the world you live in?

Is this right or wrong?

English, **used** as a first or second language in about 60 countries,
is spoken by a third of the world's population.

English, **used** as a first or second language … English, **which is used** as …	Relativsätze werden oft durch Weglassen von Relativpronomen + einer Form von **be** verkürzt.

Ask your partner: Right or wrong?

1. 'Thriller', made by the Beatles, is the world's best-selling album.
2. Mozart, born in 1756, wrote music when he was four.
3. The world's most valuable painting is the Mona Lisa, painted by Leonardo da Vinci.
4. The smallest state in the world, populated by about 1000 people, is Luxembourg.
5. One of the world's most famous tourist spots is the Colosseum, built nearly 1000 years ago.
6. Ancient Egyptian kings, called pharaohs, were buried in pyramids.
7. The most popular sport, played all over the world, is baseball.
8. The sport liked best by most Americans is football.

Now your partner asks you: Right or wrong?

9. The scientist imprisoned for writing that the earth travels around the sun was Darwin.
10. The first man sent to the moon was an American.
11. The heaviest snake in the world, found in Brazil, weighed 227 kg and was 8.45 m long.
12. The highest temperature ever recorded was 58° C in the Sahara Desert.
13. The lowest temperature ever recorded was minus 40° C in Antarctica.
14. Rice, eaten on its own or mixed with other things, is the most popular food in the world.
15. The longest sausage ever made was 9 km long.
16. The language spoken by most people in the world is English.

2. The changing world

Modern science plays a vital role in explaining how the world is changing. Pictures which are sent to earth by satellite, for instance, inform us about changes in the weather. The photos which have been taken of the earth's atmosphere reveal that the ozone layer has developed a large hole and is becoming thinner. Satellite photos that have been shown on TV have helped to inform the general public about this process, which is called global warming or the 'greenhouse effect'.

Global warming, which is caused mainly by carbon dioxide and CFC gases, means that the earth's atmosphere, which is no longer protected by the ozone layer, is warming up. Over the years, chmicals that have been used in aerosol sprays and refrigerators have caused a build-up of poisonous gases, which are known as 'greenhouse gases'. Gases that are produced by traffic, industry, heating and air-conditioning systems are also contributing to this process. These poisonous gases, which become trapped in the earth's atmosphere, act like a blanket and stop the sun's heat from escaping. Reports that have been written on global warming warn that even a small rise in temperature would have dramatic effects. The polar ice would melt faster, sea levels would rise and some coastal areas would be flooded. Hot countries would get even hotter and may eventually become totally uninhabitable.

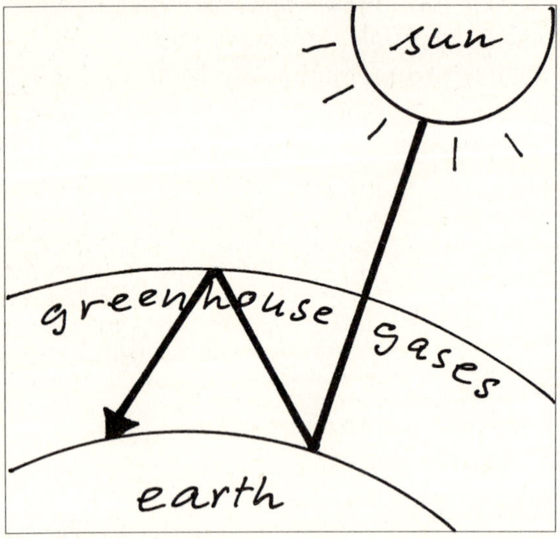

Explain what is happening to the atmospere by using these past participles:

called, caused, known, melted, produced, protected, sent, shown, taken, trapped, used, written

Pictures ____________ to earth by satellite show how the world is changing. Photos ____________ of the earth's atmosphere reveal that the ozone layer is disappearing. Satellite photos ____________ on TV have helped to raise awareness of this process, ____________ global warming. Global warming, ____________ by poisonous gases ____________ 'greenhouse gases', means that the atmosphere is becoming warmer. The atmospere, ____________ by the ozone layer, is being damaged by the sun's rays. Chemicals, ____________ in sprays and fridges and also gases ____________ by traffic and industry are causing the greenhouse effect. These gases, ____________ in the earth's atmosphere, stop the sun's heat from escaping. Reports ____________ on global warming warn that polar ice, ____________ by the sun, would cause widespread flooding.

1. The New Forest

Start your tour of the New Forest at the Information Centre in Lyndhurst.
Enjoy the video telling the story of the forest. See the work of local artists displayed in the shop. Then travel by coach into the countryside before getting off for a guided walk. Once discovered, you will love the hidden treasures of the forest.

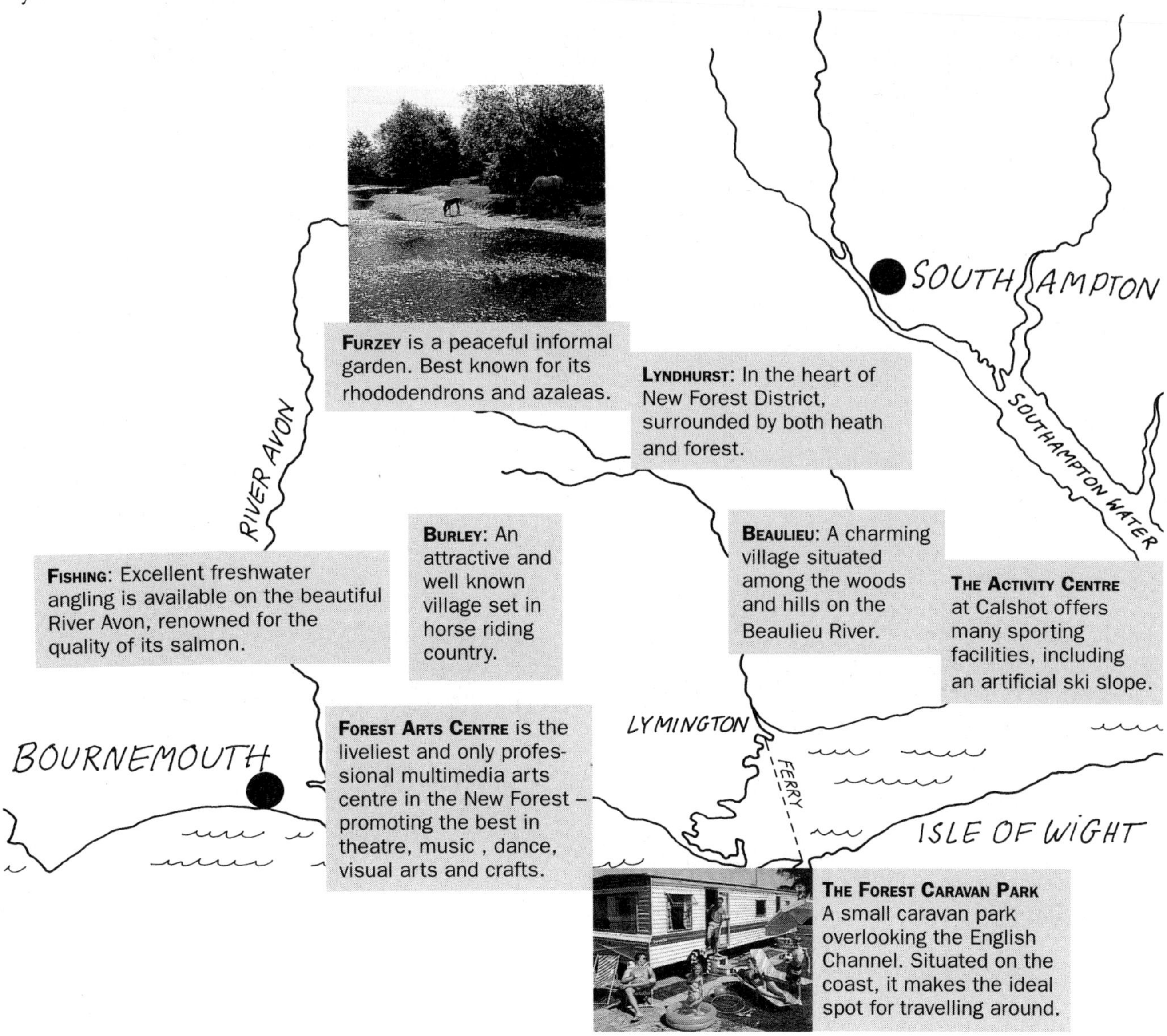

On this information leaflet about the New Forest there is not enough room for long sentences. How does the writer avoid using the following longer expressions?

Example:

It is situated among – **situated** among (Beaulieu)

1. It is surrounded by
2. It promotes
3. It tells
4. It overlooks
5. It is renowned for
6. It includes
7. Before you get off
8. It is best known for
9. It is displayed
10. It is set
11. Once you have discovered them
12. It is situated on

2. Hotels in Britain

In these advertisements participle constructions help to shorten the sentences.
Sometimes they replace verbs and sometimes they are used as adjectives.
Write out the participle constructions in full:

Castle House

☆☆☆

All rooms have a private shower and several with private toilet. All have colour television, tea-making facilities, alarm clock and central heating. A cosy family run Guest House situated just a few minutes from all of Dover's amenities and port. We are Internationally recommended. A.A. approved. Car Parking. VISA/MASTERCARD/EUROCARD.

Tariff: Bed and Breakfast from **£ 12.00** to **£ 20.00** depending on season.

1. tea-making facilities
   It has facilities to …
2. family run
3. internationally recommended
4. A.A. (Automobile Association) approved
5. depending on season

Find participle constructions in these two adverts which mean the same as these expressions:

1. It offers
2. It is situated close to the town centre
3. Up to six people can sleep there
4. It is easy to get to Dover Priory station
5. It overlooks a green park
6. It is included in the A.A. hotel list
7. The back garden is well looked-after and secluded

An attractive Victorian house offering cosily furnished rooms with central heating, tea/coffee making facilities, television lounge and private car park. Conveniently situated for Dover Priory railway station, town centre and 5 minutes by car to docks. Open all year. AA listed. ☆☆

Seaside House

☆☆☆

Fully furnished, self-catering house, situated close to town centre, sea front and station. Accommodation comprises lounge, dining room, kitchen, bathroom/toilet, separate toilet and 3 bedrooms, sleeping up to 6. Well maintained secluded rear garden. Overlooking green park.

3. Writing an advertisement

Write an advertisement for the Kingswood Hotel. Use participle constructions to shorten and combine the information.

Example: – The Kingswood Hotel is run by the Bolton family. It is a beautifully furnished small hotel.
– *Run by the Bolton family, the Kingswood Hotel* is a beautifully furnished small hotel.

– It is highly recommended. It is listed by the AA. It is personally managed by Lynne Bolton.
– It is situated close to the town centre. So visitors can easily walk to the shops.
– It overlooks the bay. That means we have wonderful views of the sea.
– Because it is set in large gardens the hotel provides peaceful surroundings to simply relax.
– Only a few miles away is the lovely New Forest. The Forest offers marvellous opportunities for walking and horse-riding.
– You will be given a warm welcome whether you stay overnight or longer.
– Terms: £ 35.00 B & B per person. This depends on the season. There are family rooms where 4 people can sleep. They cost from £ 70.

1. Where would you go?

Where would you go to have your watch repaired?

- your hair cut?
- your coat cleaned?
- your eyes tested?
- your shoes mended?
- your photos developed?
- your hair dyed?
- your washing done?
- your glasses cleaned?
- your money changed?
- a passport photo taken?

Which number would you ring to get

- something typed?
- your fortune told?
- your room decorated?
- your teeth checked?
- your car serviced?
- your oven mended?
- your windows cleaned?

to have/get something done
etwas machen lassen

HALL'S HEEL BAR
One hour service

UNISEX
Hairdressing

Scott Christie B:D:S
Dental Surgeon
64 HIGH STREET
529034

MOONEY'S
OPTICAN'S

MARTIN'S GARAGE
Services and repairs
984202

KLEENIT'S
Cleaner's

You write – we type
Tel. 601548

NEEDHAM'S
Photographer's
One hour service

NATIONAL
WESTMINSTER
BANK

Window cleaner
Phone 443005

GRAYSON'S
Watch repairs

PAINTING AND
DECORATING
Ring 223066

THE ELECTRICAL
REPAIR MAN
Tel. OFFICES
83104 SHOPS
HOUSES
Electrical Repairs

THE LAUNDRETTE
26 High St.

2. What should they do?

What should these people do?

1. Mary's TV has broken down.
   She should have it mended.
2. Mike's hair is too long. He …
3. Jane doesn't like the colour of her hair. …
4. There's a hole in Tim's shoe. …
5. The Smith's flat has not been decorated for years. …
6. Ken has got oil on his jacket. …
7. Ann's car keeps breaking down. …
8. Mrs Oldfield's windows are too high for her to clean. …
9. Barbara can't hear very well. …
10. Mr Owen can't see very well. …

3. Have you ever had it done?

Have you ever had these things done?
Ask your partner.

Have you ever had …?

your fortune told?
your hair dyed/permed?
your ears pierced?
your eyes/hearing tested?
a tooth filled/pulled out?
your lungs X-rayed?
a passport photo taken?
Do you like having your photo taken?

4. Jokes

Can you tell these jokes? Use *to have/get something done.*

1. When the clock strikes thirteen what time is it?
   Time to … (to repair)
2. Dear Father Christmas,
   I'd like a model plane, please. And I want to … my bike … and my violin … (to mend/to break)

5. Warnings

Give warnings like this: *Don't put your glasses there. You'll get them broken.*

1. Don't leave your bike there.
   You'll … it … (steal)

2. Don't play with those matches.
   You'll … your fingers … (burn)

3. Don't play there.
   Someone will … their windows … (break)

4. Don't drive so fast.
   You'll … your licence … away. (take)

What needs doing?

The windows **need/want cleaning.** = They **should be cleaned.**
Someone should clean them.

need } + -ing
want

To start you off: *empty, tidy up, make, hoover …*

1. Could I speak to Colin, please?

Barbara: Hello, Mrs Baxter.
Could I speak to Colin, please?
Mrs Baxter: Just a minute. He's in his room doing his homework. I'll get him.

Colin is **in his room doing** his homework.	Das Partizip Präsens (*-ing* Form) wird oft verwendet, um **Begleitumstände** wiederzugeben.

Make up telephone conversations like this with your partner:

– Could I speak to … , please?
– Just a minute.(S)He's in … … ing …
I'll get …

bathroom — having a shower
garden — reading
living room …

lie
stand } + *-ing*
sit

2. Busy doing nothing

Mrs Baxter:
Angela. You're just **lying doing** nothing. Can't you help me to get tea ready?

Angela:
Oh, Mum. I'm so tired. I've been … clothes all day. (stand, sell)

Mrs Baxter:
All right. Colin, you're only … TV. Come and give me a hand. (sit, watch)

Colin:
Oh, Mum. It's interesting. And I need it for school.

Mrs Baxter:
Oh, all right. Joe, you're just … out of the window. Can't you come and help? (stand, look)

Joe:
Just a minute. I'm just watching Mr Henderson. He's been … out of his window for about half an hour. (stand, look)

1. What presents has Mrs Wilson bought?

Mrs Wilson has just bought her Christmas presents. This was her list.

Ken - video	Diane - camera
Laura - book	Wayne - football
Tony - game	Josie - necklace
Alan - watch	Barbara - scarf
Mary - ring	

1. She has bought a video **for Ken.**
2. She has bought Ken **a video.**

Was dem Sprecher am **wichtigsten** ist, kommt am **Schluß** des Satzes.

Was fällt dir bei Satz 2 auf?

What has Mrs Wilson **bought** for Diane and Tony? (Am wichtigsten ist, *was* sie gekauft hat).

1. She has bought ______________________
2. ______________________

What has she got for Laura, Alan and Barbara?

1. She has got ______________________
2. ______________________
3. ______________________

What is she going to give Mary, Wayne and Josie?

1. ______________________
2. ______________________
3. ______________________

2. Who are the presents for?

Cover up the rest of this page. **Who** has Mrs Wilson bought all these presents for? Can you remember?

She has bought the video **for Ken.**
She has got …
She is going to give …

3. Birthdays

Do you like finding birthday presents for people? What sort of things do you get?

- I usually get (my mother) a/some …
- Last year I made a (scarf) for my …
  He loved it/didn't like it much.
- Once I sent/gave …
- This year I think I'll/I might buy …

buy/get/give/make/send

↓	↓
someone something	something to/ for someone

4. Show me your presents

Everyone liked the presents Mrs Wilson bought. They are showing them to their friends. What do their friends say? *(lend, play, read, show)*

Tracy: "Will you ____________ your camera, Diane?"

Ann: "Will you ____________ your new book, ____________?"

Derek and Lynne: "Will ____________ your new game, ____________?"

Suzy: "____________ your scarf, ____________?"

Wayne and Maria: "____________ your new video, ____________?"

Diane's mother asks her daughter, "Have you showed your presents **to Grandma**?"

"Have you showed ____________?" (video/your father)

"You could read ____________?" (new book/sister)

1. Will you **show me** your presents?
2. Have you **showed** your presents **to** Grandma?

Gegenstände

Person

> In Sätzen des Typs 1 wird das Augenmerk auf die ____________ gerichtet,
> in Sätzen des Typs 2 eher auf die ____________.

5. Tell me, please

Tony's friends want to play his new game.

They ask him, "Can you ____________ us how to play?" (say/tell?)

Tony ____________ that he couldn't play it himself yet. (say/tell?)

explain *say*	something to someone	*Say* wird oft von direkter Rede gefolgt, auch von *that.*
tell me/him/her/them/Tony/…		Bei *tell* muß erwähnt werden, *wem* wir etwas erzählen.

1. The Chinese New Year

The Chinese New Year starts in either January or February. It begins with the first full moon between 21 January and 19 February and the celebrations last for two weeks. It is a time for visiting friends and relatives, and giving presents.

One week before the New Year starts, the family get together to honour the god of the kitchen. They believe that this god will travel to the Emperor of Heaven to report on the family's behaviour in the last year. They burn a picture of the god so that he can leave the house. On the evening before New Year the god is welcomed back with a feast.

At New Year people only eat vegetarian meals. Some food is left outside for the dead so that they, too, will have a Happy New Year.

On New Year's Day, the last day of the two weeks, people dress up in beautiful costumes and hold street festivals with parades and dancing. A giant dragon dances at the front of the parade. Years ago fireworks were a big part of the traditional Chinese New Year. But in 1994 the government banned them because they were too dangerous. Towards the end of the celebrations lanterns are hung up to welcome the longer, warmer days of Spring. During the Cultural Revolution, from 1966–1967, religious traditions were stopped in China.

In the 1980s, however, people started celebrating the New Year again. But today many young Chinese are no longer interested in the old traditions. They have started to celebrate some Western festivals, like Christmas.

2. Time expressions

Which expressions give you information about *when* something happens, e.g. *in either January or February.* Notice where they usually appear in the sentence.

The Chinese New Year starts *in January or February.*	Adverbs of time usually at end.
At New Year people only eat vegetarian meals.	At beginning for emphasis.

3. Can you explain how the Chinese celebrate the New Year?

Read the article again until you think you can remember it very well.
Then cover it up and write as much as you can about the Chinese New Year, using these two lists.

The Chinese New Year starts	street festivals are held.
The celebrations last	people only eat vegetarian meals.
A week before the New Year starts	they were banned.
Then he goes to Heaven	during the Cultural Revolution.
He is welcomed back	lanterns are hung up.
At New Year	prefer the Western style New Year.
On New Year's Day	the family honour the kitchen god.
Years ago	New Year celebrations started again.
But in 1994	to report on the family.
Towards the end of the celebrations	the evening before New Year.
Religious traditions were banned	for a couple of weeks.
But in the 1980s	fireworks were very important.
Today many young Chinese	sometime in January or February.

4. A British Christmas

Put the words and phrases in the correct order to find out how British people celebrate Christmas.

More detailed before less detailed
At four o'clock in the afternoon

Lots of British people have Christmas parties. start/They/at about seven/and often go on until/ on Christmas Eve/early on Christmas Day, that is 25 December. Children/very early/wake up/on Christmas morning. They open the presents that Father Christmas brought them the night before. give each other presents/Adults/on Christmas morning/after breakfast/. there is/on Christmas Day/ At about one o'clock/a huge Christmas dinner. Then,/listen to/in the afternoon/most people/the Queen's Speech/on television/at three/.

5. Talking about time: at – in – on?

… Christmas	… December	… 25 December	… New Year's Eve
… the evening	… lunch-time	… the winter	… Wednesday evening
… 1998	… night	… my birthday	… half past five
… the weekend			

6. Your Christmas and New Year

Can you explain how people celebrate Christmas and New Year in your country?
How do you feel about Christmas? Would you change it?

1. The weather forecast

Good morning. You're watching Sky News. Here's Hazel with today's weather forecast for the British Isles.

Good morning. Well, it's a lovely sunny morning here in London. In the rest of the country, however, things don't look quite so good. There's a lot of rain coming in over Scotland. It will gradually move eastwards and by midday it will probably be raining all over Scotland. The afternoon will probably be better and the sun might even come through here and there. Heavy rain is also moving in from Ireland. At the moment it is raining hard in the Manchester area but they might see a little sunshine between the showers by mid-morning. This rain will move half-way across the country and by the afternoon it will be raining practically everywhere in the North. So if you don't have to go anywhere today it's best to stay at home. If you can't stay inside you'd better take a mac with you. Down in the South it's a lovely sunny morning in most places. This afternoon the sun may disappear behind the clouds for a while and there may even be a few showers here and there, but they will soon clear up. So if you're travelling around you'd better stay down South. The best weather will be around the South-East.

During the evening winds will pick up along the South coast and there will probably be a few thunderstorms in the South-West, which will move up the coast during the night.

By tomorrow it should be fine again in most parts of the country, although it will be much colder. In some parts of Scotland the thermometer will go down to below freezing. In the North and Central England temperatures will be between about two and five degrees. And in the South they will be generally above five degrees.

2. Talking about the weather

Rewrite the weather forecast by replacing the underlined words with expressions of your own.

It's a lovely morning *where I am*. In other parts of ______________, however, things aren't so good. Rain is coming __________ Scotland, and it will move ________________________. By midday it will probably be raining ______________. In the afternoon the sun might even come through ______________ in Scotland. At the moment it is raining hard __________ Manchester, but they might see a little sunshine ______________ by mid-morning. By the afternoon it will be raining ______________ of the North. So if you don't have to go ________ today it's best to stay __________. ______________ of the South it's a lovely sunny morning. This afternoon there may be a few showers in some ________ but they will soon clear up. The best weather will be __________ South-East __________.

3. Adverbs of place and direction

> – Adverbs of place tell us where something is, e.g. here in London, at home.
>
> – Adverbs of direction tell us where something is going to.
> They are often together with verbs of movement, e.g. come in, move eastwards.

Find more examples of both types of adverbs in the text and think of some of your own, too.

4. Position of adverbs of place and direction

What does the weather forecast show you about the general position of adverbs of place and direction in the sentence? Can you explain any exceptions?

Do adverbs of place usually come before or after adverbs of direction? Find examples from the text.

Write out these sentences correctly. Can you find a rule to explain your answers?

1. In Wales/My penfriend lives/in a small town

____

2. at the bus stop/Let's meet/outside the town hall

____

5. Position of adverbs of place, direction and time

Put these words in the right order.

1. this morning/lovely/here in London/It is

   It is ____

2. will move/later today/Rain/eastwards

____

3. all over Scotland/It/by midday/will be raining

____

4. will drop/Temperatures/tomorrow/in some places/to below freezing

____

What do your answers tell you about the relative position of adverbs of place, direction and time?

1. What are they like

How well do you know the person sitting next to you? Ask him or her these questions.

1. Do you generally find life easy or quite difficult?
   Do you make friends easily?
2. What sort of things are you good at? What do you do well?
3. What are you bad at? What do you do badly?
4. Are you a careful person? Do you work carefully?
   Do you handle things carefully or do you tend to break things?
5. Do you do things quickly or slowly?
   Do you speak quickly?
   Do you walk fast or slowly?
   Are you rather a fast or a slow worker?
6. Do you find school work hard?
   Do you work hard at school? Or do you hardly work at all?
7. When you go anywhere do you usually arrive early or late?
   Do you catch an early bus so you have plenty of time?
   Or do you often have to rush about?
8. How do you like to dress? Comfortably? Fashionably?
   Are most of your clothes fashionable or don't you care too much about fashion?

Now your partner asks you. Give a short description of your partner: (Jochen) generally finds life …

2. German and English

Translate into English:

1. a) Anna ist sorgfältig. b) Anna arbeitet sorgfältig.
2. a) Paul ist ein guter Fußballer. b) Paul spielt gut Fußball.
3. a) ein schnelles Auto b) schnell fahren
4. a) am frühen Morgen b) früh aufstehen

Wie hast Du die unterstrichenen Wörter übersetzt? Was fällt Dir auf?

Vervollständige diese Regeln durch Beispiele:

Viele Adverbien werden mit der Endung **-ly** von Adjektiven abgeleitet,

z.B. ______________________________

Die Adverbform von **good** ist ____________.

Manche Adjektive und Adverbien haben **gleiche Form** und **gleiche Bedeutung**,

z.B. ______________________________

A joke: What do you call a Spaniard who has been ill? – Man well.

3. Adjectives with two adverb forms: hard, late, high, near

Find out where *hard* and *hardly* are used as adjectives and adverbs in this advert.

Find out for *late* and *lately*, too.

What do the adverbs in these sentences mean in German?

1. She can jump really high.
2. Barbara is highly intelligent.
   She has a highly paid job.
3. Don't go too near the river.
4. My brother nearly fell in the
   river last week.
5. My Grandmother is nearly ninety.

> Manche Adjektive haben zwei Adverbien:
> – **Gleiche Form** und **Bedeutung** wie das Adjektiv
> – **Endung -ly** mit einer **anderen Bedeutung**.
> z.B. *hard/hardly, late/lately, high/highly, near/nearly.*

4. Hardly (ever, any)

Rewrite these sentences without changing the meaning.
Use *hardly, hardly ever or hardly any/-one/-thing*

Examples: We do not know each other very well.
We *hardly* know each other.

I don't eat many sweets.
I *hardly* eat *any* sweets.

Our teacher is not ill much.
Our teacher is *hardly ever* ill.

> **hardly any** – almost none
> **hardly ever** – practically never

1. I don't watch TV much.
2. I can't read your writing very well.
3. Helen did not say much to me.
4. We haven't got many biscuits left.
5. Not many people passed the exam.
6. Diane does not eat much.
7. Grandad doesn't go out much.

5. School reports

Mrs O'Keefe has to write reports for her class. These are her notes for Lisa and Simon.
Write their reports for her. Choose carefully between adjectives and adverbs.

Lisa
- a quick learner, but careless
- always tries to do things too fast
- almost never does her homework
- often late for school, improving lately
- makes friends easily
- a good artist

Simon
- learns quickly, works carefully
- a fast worker
- works very hard
- never arrives late
- it's hard for him to make friends
- plays the violin well

Lisa learns ______________ , but she works ______________ .

She does things too ______________ . She ______________ ever does her homework.

She ______________ for school, although ______________ she has been improving.

She is a very popular girl and finds it ______________ to make friends. She also draws very ______________ .

Simon is ______________ learner. He is ______________ , ______________ worker.

He is ______________ for school. He is rather lonely and does not make friends ______________ .

He is ______________ violinist.

6. Describing things

It often tastes horrible.
It tastes sweet.
It smells lovely.
They smell awful.
It looks beautiful.
They look soft.
It feels cold.
It feels sharp.
They sound terrible.

a needle	cats	fresh bread
new snow	honey	ice
old socks	medicine	bagpipes

taste/smell/look/feel/sound
+ Adjektiv

It tastes (lovely) and it smells (great). – A(n) …

A joke: – This soup tastes wonderful
– Yes, it sounds wonderful!

A 1

Get/be used to

Die hier zu übende Struktur *to get/be used to something/ doing something* darf nicht mit used to + Infinitiv zum Ausdruck einer früheren Gewohnheit oder eines früheren Zustands verwechselt werden. Diese Struktur wird auf Arbeitsblatt 2 geübt.
Mit dem vorliegenden Arbeitsblatt werden *to get used to* und *to be used to* zuerst isoliert, später dann zusammen geübt.

1. Getting used to Britain
Als Einführung in die erste Übung dient ein kurzes Gesprächs über Sitten und Gebräuche in anderen Ländern, an die sich der Fremde zuerst gewöhnen muß, z.B.:

L: *Has anyone ever been to a different country?*
S: ...
L: *Can you remember anything you found it hard to get used to? The food, for example? Or things people did, the way they behaved?*

Als Sprechehilfe können folgende Strukturen aufgeschrieben werden:

I found it } *hard/difficult to get used to ...*
It was
It took me a long time to get used to ...
I couldn't get used to ...

Nach einigen Schülerbeiträgen wird das Gespräch auf Großbritannien gelenkt:

L: *Has anyone ever been to Britain? Was there anything you found it hard to get used to? If you haven't been to Britain can you think of anything Germans might find it hard to get used to?*

Im Anschluß an diesen Vorspann wird der Einführungstext zu Übung 1 gelesen. Der folgende Lückentext wird im Klassenverband, in Einzel- oder Partnerarbeit, mündlich und/oder schriftlich vervollständigt.

● Lösungen
1. *She couldn't get used to eating/having bacon and eggs for breakfast.*
2. *But he soon got used to them and now he quite likes them.*
3. *She can't get used to drinking tea with milk.*
4. *She is finding it hard to get used to the British climate.*
5. *He has to get used to driving on the left. ... he has to get used to looking to the right first.*

2. Two Germans in England
Diese Übung thematisiert britische Sitten, die für deutsche Besucher ungewohnt sind.

● Lösungen:
"We're not used to shaking hands."
She is/was not used to queuing for buses.
... the English are not used to saying "good appetite."

3. Getting used to different places
In Gruppen schreiben die Schüler einige Sitten, Gebräuche oder Gegebenheiten auf, an die sie sich einmal gewöhnen mußten. Dabei können sie sich auf fremde Länder oder verschiedene Regionen innerhalb Deutschlands beziehen. Anschließend berichtet der Sprecher jeder Gruppe der ganzen Klasse, z.B.:
– *Klaus found it hard to get used to the heat in Spain.*
– *Soraya wasn't used to sitting next to boys when she first came here.*

What might visitors to Germany find it difficult to get used to?
Wiederum in Gruppen und unter Verwendung der vorgegebenen Strukturen machen sich die Lernenden Gedanken darüber, was Fremden in Deutschland schwerfallen könnte und woran sie sich gewöhnen müßten. Ihre Gedanken tragen sie der ganzen Klasse vor.

4. Getting used to living alone
In Gruppenarbeit und unter Verwendung der vorgegebenen Strukturen sammeln die Schüler Aussagen darüber, woran sich Diana gewöhnen muß. Die Gruppenbeiträge werden der ganzen Klasse mitgeteilt. Im Anschluß können die Beiträge diskutiert werden.

Vorschläge:
She'll have to get used to doing the/her own shopping/ washing/cleaning/ironing/cooking/staying in alone/ eating/watching TV/listening to music ... alone/by herself.

5. I could never get used to it
In Gruppen- oder Partnerarbeit stellen die Schüler ihre Überlegungen zusammen und tragen sie anschließend der ganzen Klasse vor. Die Beiträge können diskutiert werden.

A 2

Used to

Mit diesem Arbeitsblatt wird *used to* zum Ausdruck einer früheren Gewohnheit oder eines früheren Zustands wiederholt und geübt. *Used to* + Infinitiv kommt nur in der *past tense*-Form vor und darf nicht mit dem Ausdruck *to be/get used to* im Sinne von *to be/get accustomed to* verwechselt werden, der in Arbeitsblatt (**A 1**) behandelt wird.

1. The way things used to be
Der Text der ersten Übung kann durch ein kurzes Gespräch eingeführt werden, z.B.

L: *Have you ever thought about what happens to people who used to be famous, but aren't any more? Like some pop stars, film stars or sportspeople? This is someone called Paul McNally. Today nobody knows who he is, but he used to be a very famous boxer. Let's see what happened to him.*

In einem zweiten Schritt wird der Text gelesen und in einem dritten wird die Aufmerksamkeit auf den Merkkasten gelenkt, der Form und Funktion von *used to* in Aussage- und Verneinungssätzen (Fragesätze siehe Übung 2) erklärt.

Compare the way Paul used to live with the way he lives now.
In Einzelheiten wird Pauls früherer Lebenswandel schriftlich festgehalten und dann der Klasse vorgetragen.

● Lösungen
He used to:
earn millions of pounds a year, spend his money on expensive clothes/big houses/fast cars, buy/wear expensive clothes, live in big houses, drive fast cars, pay people to do everything for him, go out with/see his friends every night, go to night clubs, drink champagne, stay up till three in the morning, go everywhere by taxi.

He didn't use to:
save any money, do anything for himself, cook his own meals, do his own washing and cleaning, drink cheap wine, go to bed early/before three in the morning, live in a small flat, travel by bus, stay in/at home in the evenings, read, listen to music.

Paul often thinks about the past.
Unter Verwendung der Struktur *never used to* formulieren die Schüler Aussagen, die Paul selbst über sein früheres Leben gemacht haben könnte.

● Lösungen
I never used to:
save any money, cook my own meals, do my own washing and cleaning, go to bed early/before three in the morning, drink cheap wine, travel by bus, stay in/at home in the evenings, read, listen to music.

An dieser Stelle bietet sich eine Diskussion pro und contra Boxsport an. Folgende Denkanstöße werden vorgeschlagen:
Is boxing a sport or an unacceptable show of brutality?

Some views FOR boxing as a sport:
- *Boxing is wonderful entertainment.*
- *Boxers know what they are doing, about the risks they take.*
- *People should be free to do as they like, even if this means injuring themselves, even if it eventually kills them.*
- *Injuries can happen anywhere. Boxing is not more dangerous than other things, like other sports or even driving a car.*
- *A ban on boxing would send it underground.*

Some view AGAINST boxing:
- *The purpose of boxing is to injure your opponent, even if this means damaging the brain. The risk of brain damage is high.*
- *Other sports are dangerous, for instance mountaineering, but it is not the purpose of the other sports to hurt someone else, as it is in boxing.*
- *It is immoral to pay two adults to hurt each other as much as possible.*
- *A ban would not send boxing underground because professional boxing depends on money. It would just fade away.*

2. How has your life changed?
Als Vorbereitung für Übung 2 dient ein kurzes Gespräch über frühere Gewohnheiten, z.B.:

L: *And what about you? Are you a different person now from what you were a few years ago? What did you use to do? What didn't you use to do?*

Die folgenden Sprechimpulse werden an die Tafel bzw. auf Folie geschrieben:
I use<u>d</u> to ...   I didn't <u>*use*</u> to ...
Im Anschluß an die Einführung formen und üben die Schüler in Partnerarbeit Dialoge nach dem Muster der angegebenen Modelle. Über die einzelnen Aussagen kann diskutiert werden, z.B.:

A: *I used to collect stamps, but I don't any more.*
B: *Why not?*
A: *I don't know, really. I'm just not very interested.*

Ask your classmates.
In dieser Übung wird *used to* in Fragesätzen geübt. In einem Kettengespräch befragen sich die Schüler gegenseitig über frühere Gewohnheiten, z.B.:

A: *(Barbara), did you use to collect anything?*
Barbara: *No, did you?*
A: *No.*

Die befragte Person stellt die nächste Frage:
Barbara: *(Thomas), what did you use to read?* usw.

Zur Festigung schreiben die Schüler vier bis fünf Gewohnheiten auf, die ihre Klassenkameraden früher hatten bzw. nicht hatten, z.B.:
Barbara didn't use to collect anything.
Thomas used to read Batman comics.

3. Poems
Nach dem Schema der angegebenen Strukturmuster versuchen die Schüler in Einzel-, Partner- oder Gruppenarbeit Gedichte zu schreiben, die sich nicht unbedingt reimen müssen. Einige inhaltliche Vorschläge können an die Tafel geschrieben werden, z.B.:

dream about	*travelling round the world/ beautiful girls/handsome boys/ being famous/being a …*
want	*to be the best/a house/children/ lots of …*
But now	*I only want a friend who …/ I'd like/all I want is/she needs/ she's looking for/she knows …*

A 3

If III: Irreale Bedingungen

In irrealen Bedingungssätzen, bei denen die Bedingungen nicht erfüllt wurden, ist die Tempuskombination besonders schwierig. Deshalb wird zunächst der konditionale Nebensatz isoliert behandelt (Übung 1) und erst in den darauffolgenden Übungen werden Haupt- und Nebensatz zusammen betrachtet.

1. If things had been different
Die erste Übung kann folgendermaßen eingeführt werden:

L: *Do you ever feel sorry about something you've done or something you haven't done? Or something you did wrong? Do you ever think "It would have been better if I hadn't done that"? For instance you might say, "If I had worked harder I might have got better marks."*

Je nach Leistungsstand können die Schüler zu weiteren Äußerungen aufgefordert werden. Anschließend wird die Bildfolge in Übung 1 beschrieben. Dabei wird die Aufmerksamkeit hauptsächlich auf die Zeitform im *if*-Nebensatz gelenkt. Auf die Kurzformen bei der Aussprache sollte geachtet werden.

● Lösungen
1. *If Tony had gone to bed earlier he would not have got up so late.*
If Tony had not got up late he would not have missed the bus.
If Tony had got up earlier he could have caught the bus.
2. *If Tony had arrived on time he probably would not have lost his job.*
If Tony had not been late for work he might not have lost his job.
3. *If Tony had not lost his job he would not be washing up at McDonald's.*

Die Bildung des *if*-Nebensatzes kann zusammen mit den Schülern erarbeitet werden. Dazu schreibt man die vervollständigten Sätze ohne Merkkasten auf Folie. In Partner- oder Gruppenarbeit versuchen die Schüler, die Zeitform der von ihnen eingetragenen Verben zu bestimmen: *If + past perfect.* Der Merkkasten verdeutlicht die Tempuskombinationen im Konditionalsatzgefüge. Aus Gründen der Vereinfachung wird in dieser Regel auf die Möglichkeit von *would/could/might* + Infinitiv verzichtet (*If I had been born in England I would speak English*).

Bei der Gelegenheit kann man die Schüler auf die Unterschiede beim Geschriebenen und Gesprochenen hinweisen (z. B. write: would not have/could have; say: wouldn't 've/could 've).

2. Sylvia's burglar
Diese Übung beschäftigt sich mit dem gesamten Konditionalsatzgefüge. In Einzel- oder Partnerarbeit beschreiben die Schüler die Bilder.

● Lösungen
1. *If Sylvia had not left the window open the burglar would/could/might not have got in.*
2. *If the burglar had not dropped his car keys he would/could have got away faster.*
3. *If the burglar had got away faster the police would/might not have caught him.*
4. *If the police had not caught him he would/might not be in prison now.*

3. A life of crime
Der Einführungstext über Waynes kriminelle Karriere wird zunächst gelesen. Darauf spekulieren die Schüler, wie Waynes Leben hätte anders verlaufen können, z.B.:

L: *Quite a lot went wrong in Wayne's life, didn't it? Can you imagine that his life might have been different? For instance, he left school at 14. If he …?*
S1: *If he hadn't left school so early he might have got a better job.*
S2: *If he had stayed at school he could have got better qualifications.*

Anschließend werden die Lückensätze ausgefüllt.

● Lösungen

1. *If he had had/got a job he probably would not have started stealing cars or taking drugs.*
2. *If he had not taken drugs he would not have needed so much money.*
3. *If he had not broken into houses he would not have gone to prison.*
4. *If he had not gone to prison he would not have trained as a car mechanic.*
5. *If he had not done any training he would probably still be stealing cars.*

4. Your life?
In Gruppen- oder Partnerarbeit machen sich die Schüler Gedanken darüber, was in ihrem eigenen Leben oder dem ihrer Freunde, Bekannten oder Verwandten unter anderen Bedingungen hätte anders verlaufen können. Sie halten einige Ideen schriftlich fest, lesen sie anschließend der Klasse vor und diskutieren sie.

5. Poems
Nach dem Schema der vorgegebenen Muster und mit Hilfe der vorgeschlagenen Wörter versuchen die Schüler, in Partner- oder Gruppenarbeit Gedichte zu schreiben, die sich jedoch nicht reimen müssen. Die Schüler sollten ermutigt werden, nach unbekanntem Wortschatz zu suchen bzw. zu fragen.

Beispiele:

It would have been
different if she
had stayed.
But she didn't.

If I hadn't cried
he might not have
kissed me.
But I did. And he did.

If they had let me
I could have been a
famous artist.
But they didn't.

They might not have
known
if she hadn't told them
But she did.

A 4

If only + past perfect

1. If only things had been different
Zur Einführung spricht der Lehrer über einige fiktive Freunde, z.B.:

L: *Do you ever think about things that might have been different? Do you ever fell sorry you did certain things or regret that you didn't do something?*
I have a friend, for instance, who works in an office. A few years ago she had the chance to become a professional tennis player. But she didn't. And now she regrets not taking the chance. She says, "If only I had become a tennis player". (Der unterstrichene Satz wird an die Tafel geschrieben. Je nach Klasse kann auch ein Beispiel mit *hadn't* gegeben werden.)

Nach dieser Einführung wird Übung 1 in Einzel- oder Partnerarbeit, mündlich und/oder schriftlich, ausgeführt.

● Lösungen

1. *If only I had not drunk so much.*
2. *If only I had not watched that horror film.*
3. *If only I had learned Spanish.*
4. *If only I had not eaten so much cake.*
5. *If only I had got up earlier.*
6. *If only I had brought my umbrella.*
7. *If only I had not stayed up so late last night.*
8. *If only I had written the address down.*
9. *If only I had been more careful.*

2. Your regrets
Die Lernenden schreiben einige Entscheidungen oder Handlungen auf, die sie in ihrem eigenen Leben bedauern und tragen sie anschließend der ganzen Klasse vor. Über die Schüleraussagen kann diskutiert werden.

A 5

Indirekte Rede: Aussagen

Dieses Arbeitsblatt beschäftigt sich mit den sprachlichen Veränderungen, die bei der Wiedergabe direkter Rede in indirekter Rede vorgenommen werden müssen. Schwerpunkt liegt auf den Veränderungen der Tempora.
In Übung 1 kann *back-shift* vorgenommen werden, muß es aber nicht. Übung 2 verdeutlicht den syntaktischen Unterschied zwischen *say* und *tell*. Die Sätze der dritten Übung erfordern *back-shift*, da die in der direkten Rede gemachte Aussage im Moment der Wiedergabe nicht mehr zutrifft. In den Sätzen der vierten Übung drückt das *back-shift* aus, daß der Berichterstatter die in der direkten Rede gemachte Aussage anzweifelt.

1. Today's phone messages
Das Ausrichten von Telefonnachrichten kann in einem Rollenspiel geübt werden. S1 bekommt ein Kärtchen, das eine der auf dem Arbeitsblatt abgebildeten Nachrichten plus dem Namen des Anrufers enthält, z.B. Dave: "Will you tell your sister I'll ring her in about two hours, please?" S1 richtet diese Nachricht in einem simulierten Anruf an S2. S2

schließlich übermittelt die Nachricht in indirekter Rede an S3. Folgende Hilfestellung kann gegeben werden: Dave rang/Sue phoned – He/She said …

Beispiel:

S1: *Will you tell your sister I'll ring her in about two hours, please?*
S2: *Dave rang. He said he'll ring you in about two hours.*
S3: *Oh thanks.*

Fortgeschrittene Schüler können das Rollenspiel sprachlich auffüllen, z.B.:

S1: *Hello, (Markus). Is your sister in, please?*
S2: *No, I'm afraid not. Can I take a message?*
S3: *Yes, please. I'd like to talk to her about something. Will you tell her I'll ring back in about two hours, please? Do you think she'll be in by then?*
S2: *Oh yes, I think so. All right, I'll tell her. 'Bye then.*
S1: *Thanks. 'Bye.*
S2: *Dave rang while you were out. He said he'll ring again in about two hours. No, wait a minute. He rang an hour ago, so he'll ring in about an hour.*
S3: *Oh, thanks.*

Die Klasse erhält den Auftrag, etwaige Fehler bei der Wiedergabe der Nachricht festzustellen und ggf. zu korrigieren. Dabei wird auf das Merkkästchen aufmerksam gemacht.
Zur abschließenden schriftlichen Festigung werden die Lückensätze ausgefüllt.

● Lösungen
1. *Dave rang. He said he'll ('d) ring you in about an hour.*
2. *Alex rang. He said that they're (were) meeting at seven tonight.*
3. *Sue phoned. She said she has (had) bought six tickets for the match next Saturday.*
4. *Jean rang. She said she has (had) to talk to you about something.*

Was hast du bei der Wiedergabe der Telefonnachrichten verändern müssen? Mit dieser in Partner- oder Gruppenarbeit vorzunehmenden Aufgabe wird den Schülern in Erinnerung gerufen, daß neben den Tempora Personalpronomen und Adverbialbestimmungen verändert werden müssen.

● Lösungen
1. I → he, her → you, two hours → an hour
2. we → they
3. I → he
4. your sister → you

2. Say or tell?
Übung 2 erinnert an den unterschiedlichen Gebrauch von *say* und *tell.*

● Lösungen
1. *Carol said they are meeting at seven.*
2. *Brian told me that he has bought six tickets.*
3. *Dave said that he will ring tonight.*
4. *Jean wants to tell you something.*

3. Phone messages – the next day
Um die Notwendigkeit des *back-shift* zu verdeutlichen, werden für diese Übung Telefonnachrichten gewählt, deren Aussagen einen Tag alt sind und im Moment der Wiedergabe nicht mehr zutreffen.
Wie in der ersten Übung kann das Telefonieren und Ausrichten der Nachricht in einem Rollenspiel geübt werden. Schon am Ende des ersten Rollenspiels versuchen die Schüler, die sprachlichen Veränderungen zu sammeln.

● Lösungen
1. *Alex rang last night. He asked me to tell you that he would ring you last night. But you weren't in.*

Was muß deshalb verändert werden?
'll → he would, tonight → last night

In einem nächsten Schritt werden die Lückensätze ausgefüllt.

● Lösungen
2. *Sue phoned yesterday to say that she had bought tickets for the match yesterday afternoon.*
3. *Paul rang yesterday to tell you that they were meeting at his flat last night.*
4. *Ann phoned yesterday afternoon. She said she was listening to her new CDs and that if you wanted to you could go round.*

Was hast du bei der Wiedergabe der direkten Rede verändern müssen? Die sprachlichen Veränderungen werden in Partner- oder Gruppenarbeit zusammengestellt.

● Lösungen
2. *I've bought → she had bought, this afternoon → yesterday afternoon.*
3. *Maria → you, we're meeting → they were meeting, here → at his flat, tonight → last night.*
4. *I'm listening → she was listening, my → her, he wants to → you wanted to, can → could, come → go.*

4. Is it really true?
Die Lernenden versuchen in Gruppenarbeit den Bedeutungsunterschied der jeweiligen Satzpaare zu er-

kennen. Die dazugehörigen Fragen sollen sie auf die richtige Spur führen.

● Lösungen
1. *Erfreulicher ist (a).*
2. *Bei (b) hätte man eher den Verdacht auf Angeberei.*
3. *Bei (b) würde man vorsichtshalber nachfragen.*
4. *Bei (b) wäre man eher sicher, sein Geld zurückzubekommen.*

A 6

Indirekte Rede: Fragen

Dieses Arbeitsblatt beschäftigt sich mit der Umformung von Fragesätzen in der indirekten Rede. Die Übungen 1–3 behandeln Fragen mit Fragewörtern, Übung 4 hingegen bezieht sich auf Fragen ohne Fragewörter. In den Übungen 1–2 ist kein *back-shift* erforderlich, in Übung 3 die Verschiebung der Zeitform jedoch notwendig.

1. Problems with parents
In dieser Übung begegnen die Lernenden der indirekten Rede vorerst nur rezeptiv. Als Einführung dient ein kurzes Gespräch über unwillkommene Fragen z.B.

L: *Do you ever get fed up with people asking you questions? Questions like 'What are you going to do when you leave school?' 'Where have you been?' 'Who have you been with?' etc. What sort of questions do you get fed up with/ get on your nerves?*

Nach einigen Schülerbeiträgen werden die in den Sprechblasen erscheinenden direkten Fragen gelesen und den entsprechenden Leserbriefen zugeordnet.

How would you answer these letters?
Die Schüler machen einige Vorschläge, wie die drei jungen Leute ihre Lage verbessern könnten.

2. Too many questions
In Partner- oder Gruppenarbeit stellen die Lernenden die sprachlichen Veränderungen der in den Leserbriefen enthaltenen indirekten Fragen zusammen.

● Lösungen
1. *Where are you going?* → *Marion says to her friend: My mother always wants to know where I'm going. Fragezeichen fällt weg, where (Fragewort) bleibt, Personalpronomen ändert sich (you* → *I), daher auch Hilfsverb (are* → *'m), Wortstellung wie in Aussagesätzen (are you* → *I'm), Einleitung kommt hinzu (My mother always wants to know).*
2. *What are your friends like?* → *Linda says: My parents keep asking me what my friends are like. Fragezeichen fällt weg, Fragewort bleibt, Personalpronomen ändert sich (your* → *my), Wortstellung wie in Aussagesätzen, 'My parents keep asking me' kommt hinzu.*
3. *Where do your friends live?* → *Linda tells her friend: My parents want to know where my friends live. Fragezeichen fehlt, Fragewort bleibt, Personalpronomen ändert sich, 'do' fällt weg, Wortstellung wie im Aussagesatz, hinzu kommt Einleitung.*

Der Merkkasten faßt diese Änderungen zusammen.

3. Mary's problems
Im Unterschied zur vorigen Übung trifft nun das in der Frage Ausgedrückte zum Zeitpunkt der Wiedergabe nicht mehr zu. Deshalb ist *back-shift* erforderlich. In Einzel- oder Partnerarbeit werden die direkten Fragen in indirekter Rede wiedergegeben.

● Lösungen
where I had been, why I was so late, how I got home, who I was (had been) with and lots more.

4. My dream girl
In dieser Übung müssen direkte Fragen ohne Fragewörter in indirekter Rede wiedergegeben werden. Die Lückensätze werden im Klassenverband oder in Partnerarbeit vervollständigt. Fortgeschrittene Schüler können zunächst ohne Hilfe des Merkkastens versuchen, die sprachlichen Veränderungen in Form einer Regel zusammenzustellen (vgl. Übung 2).

● Lösungen
Then she asked if I had been there before.
She wanted to know if I liked dancing and whether I preferred rock or pop music.
She asked if I had been to the new disco in town.
She wanted to know if I was still at school.
She also asked if I could drive.
And then she wanted to know if I was there on my own or with my girlfriend.
And then – you'll never believe it – she asked me if I was going (there) tonight.

A 7

Indirekte Rede: Aufforderungen, Ratschläge

Dieses Arbeitsblatt behandelt die Umformung des Aufforderungssatzes in der indirekten Rede unter Verwendung des Satzmusters *tell/ask/advise/warn* + Person + *(not) to* + Infinitiv, z.B.

They tell people to get information about …
They warn you not to take …

Dos and don'ts
Das Thema „exotische Urlaubsländer" wird durch ein kurzes Gespräch eingeführt, z.B.

L: *Has anybody ever been on an exotic holiday, for instance to somewhere like Africa or India? What tips would you give someone who wanted to go there?/What sort of information would you need before you went on a holiday like that?*

Anschließend lesen die Schüler die Informationsbroschüre auf dem Arbeitsblatt und schlagen unbekannte Wörter nach. Sie erhalten eine geraume Zeit, um sich die Informationen einzuprägen. Danach wird das Arbeitsblatt zugedeckt und die Lernenden versuchen, möglichst viele der Informationen aus dem Gedächtnis wiederzugeben. Dabei bedienen sie sich folgender Strukturen, die an die Tafel bzw. auf Folie geschrieben werden:

They tell/ask/advise you to …
They tell/ask/advise/warn you not to …

● Lösungen
They tell/ask/advise you to
- *get information about passports, visas and health insurance*
- *find out how much money you are allowed to take into the country*
- *carry valuables on your person*
- *take any medicines you need with you*
- *learn some basic language*
- *buy guides and maps before you go*
- *check the opening times of shops, banks, museums etc.*
- *tell the post office you are going away*

They tell/ask/advise you not to
- *take a lot of cash*
- *take valuables with you, for instance jewelry*
- *carry a lot of cash round with you*
- *leave your valuables in the hotel room*
- *take too much luggage*
- *eat anything that is not cooked, washed in clean water or peeled*
- *expect everything to be like it is at home*
- *ignore local customs and traditions*
- *forget that you are a guest in someone else's country*

A 8

Unbestimmter Artikel

1. My dream job
In dieser Übung geht es um die Verwendung des unbestimmten Artikels im Englischen, wenn eine Person als Vertreter einer Berufsgruppe charakterisiert werden soll. Die Übung macht sich das bekannte englische Spiel *'What's my Line?'* zunutze. Zur Einführung des Spiels sammeln die Schüler englische Berufsbezeichnungen und sprechen über ihre eigenen Berufsvorstellungen, z.B.: *bank manager, bus driver, computer-specialist, doctor, farmer, hairdresser, journalist, librarian, mechanic, nurse, pilot, secretary, shop assistant, teacher, tourist guide.* Zur Durchführung des Ratespiels kommt ein Schüler nach vorne und denkt sich einen Beruf aus. Die Klasse, die in zwei Mannschaften geteilt werden kann, muß den Beruf erraten. Der befragte Schüler darf Hinweise geben, wenn die Fragenden nicht mehr weiterwissen. Die Ratephase sollte durch eine begrenzte Anzahl von Fragen (ca. 10) zeitlich beschränkt sein. Für mit *yes* beantwortete Fragen können Punkte verteilt werden.

Ask your partner
In einer weiteren Übung befragen sich die Schüler in Partnerarbeit, welcher von zwei ausgewählten Berufen ihnen lieber sei. Die Schüler sollten ihre Wahl begründen, z.B.
- *What would you rather be – a teacher or a truck driver?*
  A truck driver.
- *Why?*
  I'd like to drive long distances/wouldn't like to be with so many children all the time/a teacher has too much marking to do/…

2. A quiz
Die Verwendung des unbestimmten Artikels zur Bezeichnung der Zugehörigkeit zu verschiedenen Gruppen wird anhand eines Zuordnungsquiz geübt. Die Lösungen sind in Partner- oder Gruppenarbeit zu finden.

● Lösungen
1. *Cleopatra was an Egyptian.*
2. *Homer was a Greek.*
3. *Raphael was an Italian.*
4. *Mohammed was a Muslim.*
5. *St. Nicholas was a Catholic.*
6. *Marie Curie was a Nobel prizewinner.*
7. *Rosa Luxemburg was a Communist.*
8. *Indira Ghandi was a politician.*
9. *Barbarossa was an Emperor.*

Sollen die Regeln zusammen mit den Schülern erarbeitet werden, erscheint im Unterschied zum Arbeitsblatt das Quiz ohne Regelvorgabe auf Folie.

3. How often?
In dieser Übung geht es um die Verwendung des unbestimmten Artikels vor Zeiteinheiten. Schüler befragen sich in Partnergesprächen und berichten an-

schließend der ganzen Klasse, z.B. *(Martin) washes his hands several times a day. He brushes his teeth about* ... usw.

4. British measurements
Diese Übung enthält Mengenangaben, bei denen der unbestimmte Artikel verwendet wird. In Partner- oder Gruppenarbeit versuchen die Schüler die richtigen Antworten zu finden.

● Lösungen
1b) *a bit more than 1 1/2 kilometres*
2a) *just under a metre*
3b) *about 160 kilometres an hour*
4b) *about half a litre*
5a) *about half a kilogram*

A 9

Bestimmter Artikel

Mit diesem Arbeitsblatt wird der Gebrauch der englischen bestimmten Artikel geübt. Der Schwerpunkt liegt auf den Unterschieden zum Deutschen.

1. Advertisements and Notices
Anhand von englischen Anzeigen und Schilderaufschriften stellen die Schüler fest, in welchen Fällen der bestimmte Artikel im Gegensatz zum Deutschen nicht nötig ist. Anschließend werden die aufgefundenen Sprachbeispiele im Klassenverband, in Gruppen- oder Partnerarbeit in den Regelkasten eingetragen.

● Lösungen
1. *In der St. Georgs Kirche, zur Kirche, am Sonntag (im Deutschen wird der bestimmte Artikel bzw. der mit Präpositionen verschmolzene bestimmte Artikel verwendet).*

Im Englischen **kein** *the* vor:
1. *Monaten, Tagen, Mahlzeiten, wenn sie in **verallgemeinernder Bedeutung** gebraucht werden: in December (Text 8) on Sunday (1) for breakfast (7)*
2. *Wörtern wie school, hospital, wenn wir an die **Institutionen** und nicht an bestimmte Gebäude denken: church (1) hospital (3) school (6)*
3. *den meisten Eigennamen, z.B. von Menschen, Straßen, Brücken, Plätzen, Gebäuden: St. George's Church (1), Westminster Bridge, Downing Street (8)*
4. *abstrakten Begriffen: life (4) health (5)*
5. *einigen anderen Ausdrücken: to work, by car, by train (9), most people, in town (2)*

2. Life
In dieser Übung müssen die Schüler anhand von Satzpaaren entscheiden, ob der bestimmte Artikel benutzt werden muß oder entfallen kann. Das Ausfüllen der Lückentexte kann im Klassenverband, in Gruppen- oder Partnerarbeit erfolgen.

● Lösungen
1. a) *I only have a sandwich for lunch.*
   b) *Do you remember the lunch we had together last year?*
2. a) *My brother goes to church every Sunday.*
   b) *Where is the church that your brother goes to?*
3. a) *I am leaving school next year.*
   b) *The school I go to is great.*
4. a) *Are you looking forward to going to work?*
   b) *Yes. The work I'll be doing is very interesting.*
5. a) *The town where I was born is in the North.*
   b) *Let's go to town and look round the shops.*

3. Finding out about your partner
In dieser Übung wird mit stehenden Redewendungen gearbeitet, in denen im Widerspruch zu der vorausgegangenen Regel der bestimmte Artikel benutzt werden muß. Die Lernenden stellen sich in Partnerarbeit gegenseitig die Fragen. Sie sollten dazu angehalten werden, natürliche, kurze Antworten zu geben, z.B. *What time do you get up in the morning? – At half past six.*

● Lösungen
1. *What time do you get up in the morning?*
2. *What time do you go to bed in the week?*
3. *What time do you go to bed at the weekend?*
4. *What do you usually do in the afternoon?*
5. *How often do you go to the cinema?*
   How many times a month?
6. *Do you listen to the radio often?*
7. *Do you play the piano or the guitar?*

Die Schüler werden darauf hingewiesen, daß die stehenden Redewendungen wie lexikalische Einheiten einfach auswendig gelernt werden müssen. Im Anschluß an die Partnergespräche können einzelne Schüler der Klasse berichten, was sie über ihren Partner erfahren haben, z.B. *Kerstin gets up at half past six. In the week she goes to bed at* ... usw.

A 10

Present perfect continous

Das *present perfect continuous* wird in Übung 1 zuerst isoliert geübt, in Übung 2 dann dem *present perfect simple* gegenübergestellt.

1. Bored with life

Zunächst versuchen die Schüler, das Bild der gelangweilten jungen Frau zu deuten. Gleichzeitig wird der Text wortschatzmäßig vorentlastet, z.B.

L: *Look at the photo of this young woman. She looks bored, doesn't she? Why do you think she's so fed up?*

S: *Maybe …*

Nach einigen Schülervorschlägen, die nicht unbedingt das *present perfect continuous* enthalten müssen, wird die zu übende Form erstmals vom Lehrer verwendet: *She's bored because she's been doing the same thing for too long. Let's find out a bit more about her.* Die Schüler hören den Text zunächst in einer *listening comprehension*-Aufgabe, wobei die Arbeitsblätter noch nicht ausgeteilt werden. Der Text wird vom Lehrer vorgelesen bzw. auf Kassette dargeboten. Die Schüler machen Notizen zum Inhalt. Danach werden die Übungssätze ausgeteilt und in Gruppen- oder Partnerarbeit vervollständigt. Anschließend erhalten die Lernenden den Text, um ihre Aussagen selbst überprüfen zu können. Bei einer abschließenden gemeinsamen Besprechung kann noch einmal auf den unterschiedlichen Gebrauch von *for* und *since* hingewiesen werden.

● Lösungen

1. *She has been working in the same office since she left school.*
2. *She has been doing the same job.*
3. *She has been talking to the same people.*
4. *She has been listening to the same old stories.*
5. *She has been having lunch in the same canteen.*
6. *She has been doing the same kind of things at weekends.*
7. *She has been going to the same disco every Saturday night since she left school.*
8. *She has been going to the same place for her holidays for years.*
9. *She has been going to the same hairdresser since she was a child.*
10. *She has been wearing the same style of clothes for years.*

Die Schüler schlagen vor, wie Laura ihren Lebensstil ändern könnte.

Vorschläge:
She could/should
- *change her job/get a new job/train for something different*
- *move to a different area*
- *find different friends/join a club/start a new hobby*
- *go somewhere different for her next holiday*
- *change her hairdresser/hairstyle/try a new hairstyle*
- *change her style of clothes/dressing/get some new clothes*

Die im Merkkasten gegebene Regel für die Funktion des *present perfect continuous* sollte im Zusammenhang mit der darauf folgenden Übersetzung ins deutsche gemeinsam mit den Schülern erarbeitet werden. Sie werden feststellen, daß im Deutschen im kontinuativen Sinn gewöhnlich das Präsens benutzt wird: *Laura* ***macht*** *seit Jahren das gleiche/die gleichen Dinge.*

2. A new life

Die Funktion des *present perfect continuous* wird durch einen Vergleich mit dem *present perfect simple* deutlicher gemacht. Dazu wird das Thema der ersten Übung noch einmal aufgegriffen. Aus einem Briefauszug mit beiliegendem Foto erschließen die Schüler in Partner- oder Gruppenarbeit und unter Verwendung des *present perfect simple* Lauras neue Lebensweise.

● Lösungen

She has changed her job.
She has moved to a different town.
She has made some new friends.
She has started playing table-tennis.
She has joined a chess club.
She has changed her hairstyle.
She has changed her style of clothes/dressing.

Die Regeln im Merkkasten werden von den Lernenden selbst vervollständigt:
Wenn wir betonen wollen, wie lange etwas schon andauert, gebrauchen wir das present perfect continuous.
Wenn wir uns eher für das Ergebnis interessieren, verwenden wir das present perfect simple.

3. What about you?

Die Schüler wenden das *present perfect continuous* nun aktiv an, indem sie sich über die bisherige Dauer ihrer Hobbies befragen. In Partnerarbeit üben sie einen Minidialog nach dem vorgegebenen Muster und berichten später der Klasse, z.B.:
- *Eva plays table-tennis. She's been playing for six years.*

A 11

Future continuous

Dieses Arbeitsblatt behandelt das *future continuous* mit der Funktion, auszudrücken, daß eine Handlung zu einem bestimmten zukünftigen Zeitpunkt gerade ablaufen wird.

1. Holidays

Die Funktion des *future continuous* wird durch die Tagträume der im Arbeitsblatt abgebildeten Personen über ihre Unternehmen während ihres kommenden Urlaubs verdeutlicht. Die Texte werden im Klassenverband vervollständigt.

● Lösungen
1. *Liz won't be selling clothes. She will be lying on the beach.*
2. *Mike and Alison won't be doing homework. They will be hiking.*
3. *Jenny and Christine won't be doing people's hair. They will be sailing.*
4. *Paul won't be cleaning windows. He will be sightseeing.*
5. *Ralph and Kevin won't be driving taxis. They will be fishing.*
6. *Tracy won't be repairing computers. She will be pony trekking.*
7. *Derek won't be working in a bank. He will be touring Wales.*
8. *Charlie won't be selling cars. He will be living on a boat.*

2. Plan your own holiday in Britain
Mit Hilfe des Werbetextes stellen sich die Schüler einen Urlaub in Großbritannien vor. Im Klassenverband findet dann folgendes Kettengespräch statt: S1 fragt einen Mitschüler *Are you doing anything next week? Perhaps we could go somewhere?* Der Befragte lehnt ab mit der Begründung, er mache in der kommenden Woche Urlaub. Bei ihren Erklärungen können sich die Schüler eng an die vorgegebenen Vorschläge halten oder sie individuell verändern, z.B. durch das Nennen anderer ihnen bekannter Gebiete und Ortschaften, z.B. *I'll be sightseeing in the South of England/visiting old castles in Scotland/touring Cornwall.*

A 12

Future: present continuous

1. Simon's week
Die Textsorte „Notizen" an einer Pinnwand verdeutlicht, daß das *present continuous* u.a. auch für feste Vereinbarungen in der Zukunft verwendet werden kann.
Die Notizen werden zunächst so verbalisiert, wie sie auf dem Arbeitsblatt erscheinen, d. h. noch nicht in der Reihenfolge der Wochentage.

● Lösungen
On/Next Monday Simon's babysitting for the Browns at half past seven.
On Thursday he's having a guitar lesson at five.
On Sunday morning he's taken Mr Riley's dog for a walk.
On Saturday he's going to Tony's party at half past seven.
On Wednesday he's meeting Steve at seven o'clock.
On Saturday morning he's going to the youth club flea market.
On Friday he's playing table-tennis at half past six.

Anschließend schreiben die Schüler Simons Vereinbarungen in der Reihenfolge der Wochentage auf.

● Lösungen
2. *On Tuesday he is playing football at five.*
3. *Next/On Wednesday he is meeting Steve at seven o'clock.*
4. *Next/On Thursday he is having a guitar lesson at five.*
5. *Next/On Friday he is playing table-tennis at half past six.*
6. *Next/On Saturday morning he is going to the youth club flea market.*
7. *Next/On Saturday evening he is going to Tony's party.*
8. *Next/On Sunday morning he is taking Mr Riley's dog for a walk.*

2. Jokes
In Partner- oder Gruppenarbeit versuchen die Schüler, die zwei Teile der Witze richtig zusammenzufügen.

● Lösungen
1. → b) 2. → d) 3. → a) 4. → c)

3. Are you doing anything tonight?
Die Schüler werden aufgefordert, wahre oder fiktive Vereinbarungen mit Zeitangaben in den abgebildeten Vormerkkalender zu schreiben. Es können für einen Tag mehrere Einträge gemacht werden. Jeder Kalender wird demnach andere Einträge aufweisen:
L: *Are you as busy as Simon next week, too? What are you all doing next week? Write everything down in this diary. For example, for Monday you might put '6.00 sports centre' if you're going to the sports centre at six. On Wednesday you might put '5.30 piano lesson' if you're having a piano lesson at half past five. Some days you might have more than one thing to do. Some of you will be doing things on two or three days, others on five, six or even seven. So all your diaries will be different.*
Nach dem Ausfüllen des Vormerkkalenders versuchen die Schüler in Partnerarbeit nach dem Schema des Mustergesprächs auf dem Arbeitsblatt einen Termin zu vereinbaren. Diese Gespräche können anschließend der ganzen Klasse vorgetragen werden.

4. What are you doing next week?
Die Schüler befragen sich gegenseitig in Partnerarbeit über ihre festen Vereinbarungen für die nächste Zeit

und schreiben gleichzeitig auf, was sie über den Partner erfahren. Ausgewählte Schüler berichten anschließend der ganzen Klasse die Vereinbarungen ihrer Partner.

A 13

Future: simple present

1. A Tour of London

Dieses Arbeitsblatt behandelt das *simple present,* das ausdrückt, daß ein zukünftiges Geschehen fahrplan- oder programmäßig ablaufen wird. Die Struktur wird im Kontext einer gebuchten Londonreise geübt.
Der Eingangstext wird vom Lehrer vorgelesen oder auf Kassette dargeboten, wobei von den Schülern lediglich ein Grobverstehen erwartet wird. Es kann schon zu diesem Zeitpunkt anhand einzelner Textbeispiele auf die Funktion des *simple present* hingewiesen werden.

Would you like to go on this tour?
Nach der Textdarbietung durch den Lehrer erhalten die Schüler die Aufgabe, die Programmpunkte der Reise genauer zu erfassen und in den auf dem Arbeitsblatt abgedruckten Notizzettel einzutragen. Diese Aufgabe kann als Hörverstehensübung durchgeführt werden, indem der Text noch einmal vorgetragen wird und die Schüler gleichzeitig den Notizzettel ausfüllen. Alternativ wird der Text von den Lernenden still gelesen, und die Notizen werden in Partner- oder Gruppenarbeit gemacht. Die Lösungen werden anschließend der ganzen Klasse vorgelesen.

● Lösungen
Die Lösungen werden stichwortartig festgehalten (a), sind aber in ganzen Sätzen vorzutragen (b). Die Versprachlichung der Notizen kann verschieden ausfallen:
(a)

Sat. leave Ostend	*14.30*
arrive Ramsgate	*19.00*
Sun. leave Ramsgate	*10.00*
arrive London	*12.00*
check in	*12.00*
lunch	*13.00*
bus tour	*14.00–17.00*
walking tour of theatre district	*17.00–18.00*
set off for theatre	*19.00*
play	*20.00–22.30*
Mon. boat trip	*10.00–12.00*
lunch	*12.00–13.00*
walking tour of dockland area	*13.00–16.00*
hotel, REST!	*16.00*

(b)
On Saturday we leave Ostend at 14.30/on the 14.30 ferry.
We arrive in Ramsgate at 19.00.
On Sunday we leave Ramsgate at 10.00.
We arrive in London at 12.00.
We check in at the hotel at 12.00
We have lunch at 13.00.
We go on a bus tour/There is a bus tour from 14.00 to 17.00/that starts at two and goes on till five.
We go on a walking tour of the theatre district from 17.00 to 18.00. We set off for/go to the theatre at 19.00.
The play (starts at eight and) goes on/lasts from 20.00 to 22.30.
On Monday we have/there is a boat trip from 10.00 to 12.00.
We have/There is an hour's break for lunch from 12.00 to 13.00.
We go on/There is a walking tour of the dockland area from 13.00 to 16.00.
We go/They take us back to the hotel for a rest at 16.00.

2. Checking the details

Die in Übung 1 gesammelten Aussagen zu dem Reiseprogramm werden nun in Fragesätze verwandelt und in einem Rollenspiel geübt. In Partnerarbeit übernimmt abwechselnd der eine Schüler die Rolle des Reiseleiters, der andere die eines Reiseteilnehmers. Um Auskunft geben zu können, muß sich der „Reiseleiter" immer wieder auf den Text und seinen ausgefüllten Notizzettel beziehen. Die Antworten der „Reiseleiter" sollten in kurzen, natürlichen Sätzen erfolgen.

● Lösungen
When do we leave Ostend? – On Saturday afternoon at half past two/on the half past two ferry.
When do we arrive at Ramsgate? – Four and a half hours later/At seven.
When do we leave Ramsgate? – On Saturday morning at ten.
What time do we arrive in London? – Two hours later/At twelve.
What time do we check in at the hotel? – At twelve.
When do we have lunch? – At one.
When does the bus tour of London start? – At two.
When is the bus tour over? – At five.
When is the walking tour of the theatre district? – At/It starts at five.
What time does this walking tour finish? – At six.
How do we get back to the hotel? – The walking tour ends there.
What time do we set off for the theatre? – At seven.
When does the play start? – At eight.
How long does the play go on for? – Two and a half hours/Until half past ten.

When is the boat trip? – On Monday morning at ten.
Which river do we go on? – The Thames.
How long does the boat trip take? – Two hours/Until twelve.
What do we do after the boat trip? – Have lunch.
How long do we have for lunch? – An hour.
And then what do we do? – Go on a three hour walking tour of the new docklands area.
What time do we get back to the hotel? – At four.

In einem letzten Schritt können die Paare versuchen, ihre Dialoge nur mit Hilfe des Textes und ihrer Notizzettel zu führen, d.h. ohne die Unterstützung der in Übung 2 abgedruckten Fragen. Einige ausgewählte Dialoge werden der ganzen Klasse vorgeführt.

A 14

Nebensätze mit Zukunftsbezug: *when, as soon as, until*

Die Einheit beschäftigt sich mit der Verwendung von *simple present* und *present perfect* in Nebensätzen mit Zukunftsbezug. In den Nebensätzen der Übungen 1 und 2 steht das *simple present*, in denen der Übung 3 auch das *present perfect*. Eine Form des *will-future* ist in diesen Nebensätzen nicht notwendig, da der Zukunftsbezug schon im Hauptsatz ausgedrückt wird.

1. Finding your way around London
Mit Hilfe des Plans der Londoner Innenstadt üben die Schüler, nach dem Weg zu fragen und Wegbeschreibungen zu geben. Zur Demonstration der zu übenden Strukur werden die drei Lückentexte im Klassenverband vervollständigt.

● Lösungen
1. *Of course. Go down Charing Cross Road. As soon as you come to a crossroads turn right. The British Museum is just across the road.*
2. *Oh, yes. Just go down the Mall until you come to a big building. That's it.*
3. *Of course. Go down Whitehall and when you get to a crossroads turn left and go straight on.*

Die ausgefüllten Lückensätze dienen als Beispiele für die Regel im folgenden Merkkasten.

2. Giving directions
Nach der in Übung 1 enthaltenen Demonstrationsphase wird die Struktur nun geübt, indem sich die Schüler in Partnerarbeit abwechselnd nach dem Weg fragen. Die Dialoge sollten zuerst mündlich geübt werden. Zur Festigung kann man anschließend die Lückentexte schriftlich vervollständigen lassen.

● Lösungen
1. *Turn right. As soon as you are on the other side of the river turn left. Go straight on until you come to a big crossroads. Keep going straight on. When you get to the next crossroads turn left.*
2. *Go down Whitehall. As soon as you get/come to Trafalgar Square turn right. Go on until you get/come to a big crossrads. Go straight on. When you get/come to the next crossroads go straight on/across. St. Paul's is on your left.*
3. *Go straight on down Cannon Street. When you get/come to a big crossroads go straight on. Don't go down to the river. Go on until you get/come to another (big) crossroads. Again, go straight on. Keep going until you get/come to Trafalgar Square. When you get/come to Trafalgar Square turn left down Whitehall until you get/come to a T-junction. Westminster Abbey is across the road.*
4. *Go straight on down Cannon Street until you get/come to a big crossrads. Turn left. When you get/come to the river cross Blackfriars Bridge. As soon as you are on/get to the other side of the river turn right. When you get/come to a big crossroads go straight on. Keep going until you get/come to the next big crossroads. Then turn right onto Westminster Bridge. Go straight on until you get/come to another big crossroads. Go straight on until you get/come to/reach the end of Birdcage Walk. Buckingham Palace is in front of you.*

Der bestimmte Artikel (nicht auf dem Arbeitsblatt)
Die Hauptsehenswürdigkeiten Londons bieten Gelegenheit, kurz an den Gebrauch des bestimmten Artikels zu erinnern:

Trafalgar Square	The Mall
Buckingham Palace	The Houses of Parliament
Westminster Abbey	The British Museum
Westminster Bridge	The Tower of London
St. Paul's Cathedral	Tower Bridge

3. Moving to London
Drei Beispielsätze und ein Merkkasten erinnern daran, daß nach *as soon as*, *when* und *until* in Nebensätzen, die sich auf die Zukunft beziehen, neben dem *simple present* auch das *present perfect* stehen kann. Das *present perfect* steht, wenn die Vorzeitigkeit gegenüber der zukünftigen Handlung im Hauptsatz besonders betont werden soll (z. B. *I can't give you an adress until I've found a flat*). Sonst genügt im Nebensatz das *simple present*, da die zeitliche Beziehung von Haupt- und Nebensatz durch die Konjunktionen ausgedrückt wird.

Die auf die Demonstrationsphase folgenden Minidialoge werden in Partnerarbeit geübt. Anschließend können die Lücken der Dialoge schriftlich ausgefüllt werden.

● Lösungen
Pauline: Of course. But not until I have got a permanent address.
Jenny: I'll come and stay with you when I'm on holiday.
Pauline: Great. I'll write as soon as I have found a flat.
Derek: I can't come to see you until I have saved some money.
Pauline: All right. Let me know when you have got enough.
Pauline (to Ann): We'll talk about it when you come to see me.
Pauline (to Sue): Great. Write to me as soon as you know the date.

A 15

Future perfect

1. The year 2100
Das *future perfect* wird anhand von Zukunftsprognosen geübt. Das Arbeitsblatt stellt hypothetische Aussagen zusammen über Ereignisse, die im Jahre 2100 eingetroffen sein werden oder nicht. In Partnerschaft lesen sich die Schüler die Prognosen abwechselnd vor und reagieren sprachlich darauf. Mögliche Antworten wären *Yes, I agree/think so, too/No, I disagree/don't agree/It's possible, but .../Maybe ...*
Anschließend wird jede Prognose im Klassenverband von einzelnen Schülern vorgelesen. Je nach Klasse kann man entweder zu jeder Prognose lediglich ein paar Schülerreaktionen sammeln oder aber ausführlicher darüber diskutieren lassen.
In einem abschließenden Schritt stellen die Lernenden in Gruppen- oder Partnerarbeit schriftlich ihre eigenen Vorstellungen über das Jahr 2100 zusammen. Man sollte darauf aufmerksam machen, daß *will not* normalerweise in der geschriebenen Sprache, *won't* hingegen in der gesprochenen Sprache verwendet wird.

2. The world's population
Diese Übung kann durch kurze Spekulationen über die Entwicklung der Weltbevölkerung eingeleitet werden, z.B.: *Let's think about one of the world's biggest problems – its population. Do you think the number of people living in the world will have increased or not by the year 2100? Today the world's poplation is about 5 billion. How many people do you think will live in the world by 2050?*
Danach wird die graphische Darstellung in Partner- oder Einzelarbeit interpretiert und versprachlicht.

● Lösungen
In 1950 the world's population was about 2.5 billion. In 1992 it was about 5 billion. Scientists say that by 2025 it will have increased to about 8 billion and by 2050 it will have grown to about 10 billion.

Weitere Übungsmöglichkeit (nicht auf dem Arbeitsblatt):
Die Lernenden spekulieren über ihr eigenes Leben in etwa zwanzig Jahren und verwenden dabei das future perfect:
What do you think your life will be like in twenty years time?
What will or won't you have done?
Folgende Strukturen können als Hilfestellung angeboten werden:
I'll probably have .../probably won't have/might (not) have ...)

Mögliche Antworten:
I'll probably have/probably won't have/might (not) have got married/had children/got a job/moved to ...

A 16

Infinitiv mit *to* nach *for* + Objekt

Für die Struktur *for* + Objekt + *to*-Infinitiv verwendet man im Deutschen verschiedene andere Konstruktionen, z.B. – wie in dem vorliegenden Arbeitsblatt – einem Relativsatz mit einem modalen Hilfsverb: *Clean beaches for you to swim* – saubere Strände, an denen Sie schwimmen können.

1. Holidays
Ein Werbeposter der Ferienanlage Sunnydale Camp ruft die zu übende Struktur in Erinnerung. Der Werbetext wird zuerst gelesen, dann wird kurz über die Ferienanlage gesprochen, z.B.:
L: *Would you like to go to Sunnydale for your holiday? Why/Why not?*
What type of holiday do you prefer? What kind of holidays don't you like? usw.
Der Merkkasten erklärt Form und Inhalt der Struktur.

Would you be able to work for an advertising agency?
Die Schüler werden aufgefordert, sich als Werbefachleute zu betätigen. In Gruppen- oder Partnerarbeit und mit Hilfe des angegebenen Wortschatzes versuchen sie analog zu dem ersten Werbetext je ein weiteres Poster für die beiden vorgestellten Ferienanlagen zu entwerfen. Die Sätze der Werbetexte müssen die zu übende Struktur enthalten, inhaltlich können sie jedoch relativ frei gestaltet werden, z.B.:

A playground for children to enjoy themselves/play/relax in/get to know other children/...
Aus Zeitgründen kann man von jeder Gruppe bzw. von jedem Paar auch nur je einen Werbetext verlangen.

● Lösungsvorschläge

1. ***Sunnylands holiday camp***
   Beautiful beaches for you/people to swim or just relax.
   A playground for children to enjoy themselves.
   A disco for you/young people to learn all the latest dances.
   A kiosk for you to buy your favourite newspapers and magazines.
   Courses for you to learn sailing and surfing.
   Organised games for you to get to know people.
   A campsite for you to put up your tent.
   Lots of interesting places for you to visit.
   Boats for you to hire.

2. ***Good Fun holiday village***
   Lovely beaches for you to swim or just lie on the sand.
   Bikes for you to hire.
   A games room for you to play table-tennis and billiards.
   A cinema for you to see your favourite films.
   A library for you to borrow books.
   A café for you to have a quick snack.
   A laundrette for you to do your washing.

A 17

Infinitiv mit *to* nach Adjektiven

Diese Einheit behandelt die Struktur Adjektiv + *to*-Infinitiv in den folgenden Verbverbänden:

- *It's* + Adjektiv + *to*-Infinitiv (*It's helpful to speak different languages.*)
- Nomen + Form von *be* + Adjektiv + *to*-Infinitiv (*Animals are great to work with.*)

Die Struktur wird im Rahmen des Themas „Berufe" geübt. Zur Einführung werden die Schüler und Schülerinnen nach ihren Berufswünschen gefragt, wobei so viele Berufsbezeichnungen wie möglich gesammelt werden, z.B.:

L: *Have you thought of what you want to be when you leave school yet?* (Nach einigen Schülerbeiträgen):
Does anyone want to be a (mechanic) or a ...? Why/Why not?

1. What job do I do?
In Partnerarbeit stellen sich die Schüler abwechselnd Fragen 1–20. Eine Reihe von Fragen lassen mehrere Antworten zu.

● Lösungsvorschläge

1. *Teacher*
2. *Air hostess/tourist guide/pilot*
3. *Air hostess/tourist guide/hotel manager/taxi driver*
4. *Waiter/shop assistant/hotel manager*
5. *Model/air hostess*
6. *Pilot*
7. *Astronaut*
8. *Doctor/nurse/teacher*
9. *Hairdresser*
10. *Night watchman*
11. *Mechanic*
12. *Fashion designer*
13. *Vet*
14. *Farmer/builder*
15. *Fashion designer/cook/gardener*
16. *Fashion designer/cook*
17. *Builder/farmer*
18. *Bank manager/employer*
19. *Taxi driver*
20. *Secretary*

Der Merkkasten erklärt Form und Bedeutung der Struktur.

2. What do I do?
Dieses Ratespiel kann in Gruppen oder als Mannschaftswettbewerb im Klassenverband durchgeführt werden. Jeweils ein Schüler beschreibt seinen fiktiven Beruf durch Nennung einer dafür notwendigen Fähigkeit, Fertigkeit oder Charaktereigenschaft und unter Verwendung der zu übenden Struktur, z.B.: *In my job it's important to like making things with your hands be creative.*
Die Schüler dürfen ihre Rateversuche durch Fragen einengen, wie etwa *Do you work outdoors/have to drive a lot/have to be good-looking?* Die Anzahl der Fragen wird auf 4–6 begrenzt.

3. What jobs do they do?
In Gruppen oder mit einem Partner versuchen die Schüler, die in den Namen versteckten Berufe herauszufinden.

● Lösungen

1. *Pilot*	5. *Policeman*
2. *Doctor*	6. *Footballer*
3. *Photographer*	7. *Postwoman*
4. *Gardener*	

Anschließend erfinden die Schüler selbst Namen, in denen Berufe versteckt sind.

A 18

Infinitiv mit *to* nach bestimmten Verben

Dieses Arbeitsblatt beschäftigt sich mit den wichtigsten Verben, nach denen nur der Infinitiv mit *to* stehen kann.

1. A questionnaire
Der Fragebogen wird in Partnerarbeit ausgefüllt: Partner A befragt Partner B und trägt dessen Antworten stichwortartig ein, z.B. 1) *be a pilot, have a family* 2) *drive a car, sail.* Danach wird Partner A befragt. Anschließend kann ein Klassenprofil erstellt werden: Mit Ausnahme der ersten beiden Fragen wird festgestellt, wieviele Schüler auf die jeweilige Frage mit *yes, often, sometimes* usw. geantwortet haben. Dabei geht jeder Schüler von den Antworten aus, die auf seinem Arbeitsbogen stehen, d.h. von denen seines Partners.
Im Merkkasten werden die Verben alphabetisch aufgelistet, nach denen der Infinitiv mit *to* steht.

2. What I want in life
Mündlich und/oder schriftlich machen sich die Schüler einige Gedanken über ihr eigenes Leben. Sie sollten ermutigt werden, nach unbekanntem Wortschatz zu suchen bzw. zu fragen.

3. A joke
Um den als Lückentext dargebotenen Witz zu verstehen, müssen die beiden Lücken wie folgt ausgefüllt werden: *planned to go – forgot to close*

A 19

Infinitiv mit *to* nach Verb + Objekt

1. Running away from home
Ein Ausschnitt aus einem Zeitungsartikel über ein von zu Hause weggelaufenes Mädchen bildet den Einstieg in diese Einheit. Die Schüler können zunächst in einem kurzen Gespräch über die Motive des Mädchens spekulieren, dann erarbeiten und formulieren sie mit Hilfe der im Arbeitsblatt abgedruckten direkten Aussagen und Lückensätze die wirklichen Gründe.

● Lösungen
"Mum tells me to change my hairstyle".
"Mum tells me not to go out so often at night."
"Dad asks me not to play my music so loud."
"He warns me not to leave school without good qualifications."
"Grandma asks me to go and see her more often."
"You don't/won't allow me to go on holiday with my friends."
"One teacher expects me to go to college."
"Another teacher doesn't want me to go to college, but to get a job."
"Mum wants me to be a teacher."
"Julie tells me not to get a job yet, but to go and see the world first."
"Mike doesn't want me to go away from home."
"Uncle advises me not to wait too long before I decide."

Ein Merkkasten verdeutlicht die Bildung der Struktur, Objekt + Infinitiv mit *to* nach bestimmten Verben.

Zum Abschluß der Übung machen die Schüler Vorschläge, wie Mary ihre Lage verbessern kann. Vokabelhilfen: *talk/listen to each other more, be more tolerant/thoughtful/considerate.*

2. Other people
In Gruppen oder mit einem Partner überlegen die Schüler, was sie sich gern von einem anderen Menschen wünschen, z.B.:
I want/I'd like my friend to go to football matches with me.
my brother to stop talking about computers all the time.
I don't want people to use my things without asking.
usw.
Danach machen sie – zuerst schriftlich, dann mündlich – Aussagen darüber, was sie bei anderen Menschen nicht mögen, z.B.:
I hate it when people want/ask/tell/expect me to get my hair cut/wear different clothes/tidy my room/turn my music down/lend them things/ tell them everything
... not to watch so much TV/go out so much/wear certain things

I hate it when people don't want/allow me to wear what I like/go where I like/do what I want/do things when I want to/go out with who I want/stay out ...

A 20

Infinitiv oder *-ing* Form nach bestimmten Verben

Diese Einheit beschäftigt sich mit den wichtigsten Verben, auf die Infinitiv oder Gerundium folgen kann.

1. Brothers and sisters
Die erste Übung wird durch ein kurzes Gespräch über die Verschiedenartigkeit von Geschwistern eingeführt, z.B.:

L: *How many of you have brothers or sisters? Are they like you or are they very different?*
S1: *My sister's very different (from me).*
S2: *My brother's (a bit/lot) like me.*
usw.

Anschließend werden die Texte gelesen. Die folgenden Fragen werden dann unter Verwendung der angegebenen Strukturen zuerst schriftlich beantwortet, danach vorgelesen, z.B. *Brian is like me because he enjoys doing quiet things and because he avoids doing energetic things. I'd prefer Pam as my friend because she loves going out with friends.* usw.

2. I just love doing grammar
In dieser Übung erfolgt die Bewußtmachung. In einem ersten Schritt erstellen die Schüler in Partner- oder Gruppenarbeit aus den drei vorausgegangenen Personenbeschreibungen zwei Listen von Aussagen, wobei die erste Liste Verben + *-ing* Formen enthält und die zweite Verben + Infinitive. Daran anschließend vervollständigen sie eine vorgegebene Regel.

● Lösungen
Verbs followed by the -ing Form
I like reading. (Brian)
I don't mind being alone. (Brian)
I also like making things. (Brian)
I avoid doing energetic things. (Brian)
I prefer moving around. (Pam)
I like being with other people. (Pam)
I love going out with friends. (Pam)
I hate following routines. (Mary)
I can't stand doing the same things. (Mary)

Verbs followed by the infinitive
I like to get up early. (Pam)
Sometimes I want to be with other people. (Mary)
Sometimes I prefer to be on my own. (Mary)
I'd hate to plan everything. (Mary)

These verbs can be followed by the -ing form or the infinitive: like, prefer, love, hate.

In einem zweiten Schritt werden wiederum aus den Personenbeschreibungen Aussagen gesammelt, die allgemeine Vorliegen oder Abneigungen ausdrücken.

● Lösungen
I love going out with friends.
I hate following routines.
I like being with other people.
I prefer moving around.

Der Merkkasten schließt die Bewußtmachungsphase ab.

What sort of person are you?
Mit Hilfe der angegebenen Verben und Strukturen beschreiben sich die Schüler nun selbst. Ihre Aussagen werden ohne Namensnennung auf ein separates Blatt geschrieben. Die Schüler können die in den drei Ausgangstexten enthaltenen Vokabeln verwenden, sollten aber ermutigt werden, nach unbekanntem Wortschatz zu suchen bzw. zu fragen. Alle Beschreibungen werden eingesammelt und derart wieder ausgeteilt, daß kein Schüler sein eigenes Blatt erhält. Einzelne Schüler lesen nun die ihnen vorliegenden Texte vor und die Klasse versucht, den Verfasser bzw. die Verfasserin zu erraten.

3. Some Jokes
In dieser Übung wird die Struktur *keep/stop + -ing* Form in Partnerarbeit anhand einiger Witze wiederholt. Die beiden einleitenden Witze dienen zur Erklärung der Struktur. In einem ersten Schritt vervollständigt Partner A die Witze 1–4 schriftlich und Partner B die Witze 5–8. In einem zweiten Schritt liest jeder Schüler seinem Partner seine vier Witze vor.

● Lösungen
1. *Doctor, doctor, I keep thinking I'm invisible.*
2. *Because people kept talking behind his back.*
3. *Please stop shouting, I haven't started yet.*
4. *I keep thinking it's Monday.*
5. *Doctor, doctor, I keep losing my memory.*
6. *Doctor, doctor, I keep thinking I'm a Kangaroo.*
7. *That's because my father has stopped helping me.*
8. *No, they kept asking me …*

A 21

Infinitiv und *-ing* Form nach *forget, remember, stop, try*

Auf diesem Arbeitsblatt werden die wichtigsten Verben wiederholt und geübt, bei denen sich die Bedeutung ändert, je nachdem, ob sie von einem Infinitiv oder einer *-ing* Form gefolgt werden. *Forget* und *remember* werden in Übungen 1–3 behandelt, *stop* in Übung 4 und *try* in Übung 5.

1. Did you remember to do it?
Diese Übung beschäftigt sich mit den beiden Verben *remember/forget* + Infinitiv. In Partnerarbeit und mündlich befragen sich die Schüler, welche Besorgungen, deren Erledigung sie ihrem Partner versprachen, sie vorgenommen und welche sie vergessen haben. Dazu kreuzt Partner A auf seiner auf dem

Arbeitsbogen abgedruckten Liste drei Besorgungen an, die er erledigt hat. Partner B geht analog vor. Da die Schüler die Eintragungen ihrer Partner nicht sehen, entsteht durch die *information gap*-Aufgabe eine reale Kommunikationssituation.

What did you both forget to do?
Zur Festigung hält jeder Schüler schriftlich fest, was er und sein Partner vergessen haben.

2. I always forget it
Mündlich und/oder schriftlich geben die Schüler einige ausgewählte Beispiele dafür, was sie selbst, Verwandte oder Bekannte immer wieder vergessen, z.B. *I always forget to write my homework down/clean my teeth/buy biro refills/set my alarm/...*
My father can never remember to buy stamps/get petrol/ get coins for the shopping trolley/...

Ask your partner.
In diesem Schritt befragen sich die Schüler in Partnerarbeit, welcher Methoden sie sich zur Gedächtnissteigerung bedienen, z.B.

You: *How do you remember to do your homework?*
Partner: *By writing it down. And you?*

Write down some things you must remember to do in the next few days.
In Einzelarbeit halten die Schüler schriftlich fest, woran sie sich in den nächsten Tagen erinnern müssen und was sie nicht vergessen dürfen. Einige Schüler können ihre Aufschriebe vorlesen.

3. I remember doing it
Unter Verwendung der zu übenden Strukturen schreiben die Schüler einige Dinge auf, an die sie sich gut erinnern bzw. die sie nie vergessen werden, z.B.: *I remember learning to read. I will never forget breaking my leg while I was skiing.*
Die unterschiedliche Bedeutung von *remember/forget* + Infinitiv und + Gerundium wird zusammen mit den Lernenden erarbeitet, indem die beiden Auswahlantworten richtig in die vorformulierten Regeln eingesetzt werden:

remember / forget } to		remember / forget } -ing
Für etwas, was → *beabsichtigt* ist.	Handlung	← Für etwas, was *schon passier t* ist.

4. Stop
Die Bilder werden mündlich und/oder schriftlich beschrieben.
● Lösungen
1. *Carol stopped to eat some chocolate.*
   Sue stopped eating chocolate ages ago.
2. *Brian stopped smoking two years ago.*
   Eric stopped to smoke a cigarette.
3. *Lynne stopped buying coke a few months ago.*
   Diane stopped to buy some coke.

5. Try
Zur Verdeutlichung des unterschiedlichen Gebrauchs von *try* + Infinitiv und *try* + Gerundium versuchen die Schüler, Ratschläge für die angegebenen Probleme zu finden. Die Minidialoge werden in Partnerarbeit durchgeführt. Abwechselnd übernehmen die Partner die Rolle der gesprächseröffnenden und der ratschlaggebenden Person.

● Lösungen
1. *Try to (go to) sleep.*
2. *Try reading a boring book.*
3. *Try being late yourself.*
4. *Try to understand their feelings.*
5. *Have you tried using cassettes?*
6. *Just try to relax.*

A 22

Infinitiv oder *-ing* Form nach Verben der Sinneswahrnehmung

1. Aren't these Earth people funny?
Die Thematik der ersten Übung – die Erde aus der Sicht von Marsmenschen – kann durch ein kurzes Gespräch eingeführt werden, z.B.:

L: *Have you ever thought how funny we might look to someone from Mars – a Martian? All the funny things we do.*
Imagine you have just come to Earth from Mars for a visit – to have a look around. What might you find strange?

Nach einigen Schülerbeiträgen werden die 17 Aussagen der Marsmenschen leise gelesen. Dann wird die Modellaussage (*We watched some girls ...*) interpretiert, wobei die zu übende Struktur noch nicht verwendet werden muß, z.B.: *It was a/Someone was watching television.* Sie wird jedoch durch ein Lehrerecho in Erinnerung gerufen: *They saw someone watching television, didn't they?*

In einem weiteren Schritt lesen einige Schüler die Sätze 1–17 vor. Diese werden dann im Klassenverband ohne Verwendung der Strukturen interpretiert, z.B.:

S1: (Liest) *We watched some people go into a big building … go out again.*

S2: *Shopping – someone went shopping.*

Anschließend werden mit Hilfe des Merkkastens vorläufig nur die Formen der Strukturen bewußtgemacht.

Der Bedeutungsunterschied zwischen den beiden Strukturen wird zusammen mit den Lernenden erarbeitet. Dazu ordnen die Schüler in Partner- oder Gruppenarbeit die 17 Aussagen in zwei Listen unter dem Gesichtspunkt der Form – Infinitiv oder Partizip.

● Lösungen

Partizip Präsens:
2, 4, 5, 6, 10, 11, 13, 14, 15, 17.
Infinitiv:
1, 3, 4, 5, 7, 8, 9, 10, 11, 12, 16.

Dann wird der Bedeutungsunterschied herausgearbeitet. Das Partizip Präsens wird verwendet, wenn der Ablauf einer Handlung betont werden soll oder nur ein Teil der Handlung wahrgenommen wurde. Der Infinitiv hingegen drückt aus, daß ein Vorgang insgesamt erfaßt wurde. Dies ist vor allem bei Einzelhandlungen von kurzer Dauer der Fall.
Beispiel:

– 6. *We saw people putting things into their mouths with metal instruments.*

Die Menschen aßen immer noch, als wir wegschauten.

– 9. *We watched a man put something white into a yellow box on the wall.*

Diese Handlung kam zu ihrem Ende, bevor wir wegschauten.

2. What did the Martians see?

In dieser mündlich und/oder schriftlich vorzunehmenden Übung interpretieren die Schüler die Wahrnehmungen der Marsmenschen diesmal unter aktiver Verwendung der zu übenden Strukturen und mit Hilfe des angegebenen Wortschatzes.

● Lösungen

1. *They saw people go shopping.*
2. *They heard cars driving around all night.*
3. *They saw people switch lights off and go to bed.*
4. *They heard birds singing. They saw them fly over their heads.*
5. *They felt the sun warming their faces. They felt the rain falling on them. They saw people stop to put umbrellas up.*
6. *They saw people eating.*
7. *They watched a woman light a cigarette.*
8. *They heard a phone ring. Then they saw someone answer it.*
9. *They watched a man post a letter.*
10. *They smelled rubbish burning.*
11. *They saw people playing football/a football match.*
12. *They felt insects bite them.*
13. *They saw people wearing personal stereos.*
14. *They heard music coming out of loudspeakers.*
15. *They watched people skiing.*
16. *They saw a boy and girl kissing.*
17. *They watched two men boxing.*

3. Through Martian eyes

Die Schüler nehmen die verfremdende Sichtweise der Marsmenschen an und stellen in Gruppenarbeit und unter Verwendung der zu übenden Strukturen Aussagen über das seltsame oder lustige Gebaren der Erdenmenschen zusammen.

4. A limerick

Der Limerick soll die Kreativität der Schüler anregen, indem diese mit den zu übenden Strukturen in Gruppen- oder Partnerarbeit lustige oder merkwürdige Sätze bilden.

5. Some jokes

Durch Ausfüllen der Lücken können die Schüler die folgenden zwei Witze erzählen:

Teacher: *I hope I didn't see you look(ing) at Andy's test paper, Mike?*
Mike: *I hope you didn't, too.*

Mary: *I hear your boyfriend's a bad driver.*
Jean: *Yes. Even the lights go white when they see him coming.*

A 23

Partizip Präsens als verkürzter Relativsatz

Mit diesem Arbeitsblatt wird das Partizip Präsens nach einem Nomen als Ersatz für einen Relativsatz wiederholt und geübt.

1. Who is it?

Das Thema 'Flughafen' kann durch ein kurzes Gespräch eingeleitet werden, z.B.:

L: *Has anyone ever flown to an English-speaking country? Which airport did you arrive at? Could you understand everything? Were there any problems? What did you do when you arrived?* usw.

Die Übung basiert auf einem kombinierten Bild-Text-Rätsel. In einem ersten Schritt versucht jeder Schüler zunächst für sich allein, die auf dem Arbeitsblatt abgebildeten Personen mit dem richtigen Namen zu versehen.

In einem zweiten Schritt überprüfen die Schüler in Partnerarbeit, ob sie die Lösungen gefunden haben. Dazu stellen sich die Partner abwechselnd folgende sechs Fragen.

● Lösungen
Who's the man wearing the raincoat? – Frank
Who's the girl drinking tea? – Alison
Who's the boy wearing the anorak? – John
Who's the woman sitting on the left of Frank – Sandra
Who's the girl carrying the umbrella? – [illegible]
Who's the other girl eating crisps? – [illegible]

Anschließend wird den Lernenden Form und Funktion der Struktur bewußtgemacht:
Instead of the 'man wearing' we could say 'the man who is wearing'. Was ist der Unterschied? *'The man wearing'* ist kürzer und klingt geschliffener.

2. Would you know what to do?
In der ersten Übung erschien das Partizip Präsens lediglich als verkürzte Form der Struktur *who + present continuous.* In der zweiten Übung wird die Funktionsbreite des Partizip Präsens erweitert: Es kann außer *who* die Relativpronomen *which* und *that* ersetzen und außer Verben im *present continuous* auch solche im *simple present* (*People who live in Europe ... – People living in Europe ...; There is a board which/that gives information ... – There is a board giving information ...*).
In einem ersten Schritt der Übung versprachlichen die Schüler die im Arbeitsblatt abgebildeten Hinweisschilder unter Verwendung unverkürzter Relativsätze.

● Lösungen
People who live in Europe have to go to/through gate 1.
There is a board which gives information about hotels.
Der folgende Merkkasten faßt die Möglichkeiten der Relativsatzverkürzung durch das Partizip Präsens zusammen.
In einem zweiten Schritt versprachlichen die Schüler in Einzel- oder Partnerarbeit weitere Hinweisschilder, dieses Mal jedoch unter Verwendung verkürzter Relativsätze.

● Lösungen
Those travelling to Ankara should/have to go to/through gate 5.
People waiting for a plane should wait in the transit lounge.
There are taxis waiting at the taxi stand.
There are buses to town leaving from outside the main entrance.
There are trolleys standing by the meeting point.
Anyone visiting the town/place for the first time can buy/get maps here.
Anyone needing a hotel/hotel information should go to/look at/read the hotel information board.
People staying at the Mayfair Hotel should inquire/ask at the information desk.

A 24

Partizip Perfekt als verkürzter Relativsatz

1. How much do you know about the world you live in?
In dieser Übung wird das Partizip Perfekt in seiner Funktion als verkürzter Relativsatz im Kontext „Allgemeinwissen" wiederholt und geübt. Als Einstieg, in dem die Struktur schon verwendet wird, dient ein kurzes Gespräch über den Stellenwert der englischen Sprache in der Welt:

L: *Today we're going to think a bit about the world we live in. Let's start with the language that so many people in the world can speak – English. Some people speak it as a first language, for instance in Britain, most of North America and Australia. Some learn it as a second language, for instance in ...*
S: *India, Pakistan, some parts of Africa ...*
L: *How many people do you think speak English – half the world's population, a quarter of it, a third?*

Nach einigen Schülerbeiträgen wird folgender Beispielsatz an die Tafel bzw. auf Folie geschrieben:
English, used as a first or second language in about 60 countries, is spoken by a third of the world's population.

L: *Look at this part of the sentence* (unterstreicht *used as a first or second language*). *How else could you say it?*
S: *Which is used as a first or second language.*
L: *What's the difference?*
S: *Without 'which' it's shorter.*

Der anschließende Merkkasten verdeutlicht die Form des verkürzten Relativsatzes.

Ask your partner: Right or wrong?
Die Struktur wird mittels eines Quiz geübt: Partner A liest die Aussagen 1–8 vor und fordert seinen Partner auf, sie als richtig oder falsch zu bewerten und ggf. zu korrigieren. Entsprechend geht Partner B mit den Aussagen 9–16 vor. Die Ergebnisse werden in Notizform festgehalten. Im Anschluß an die Partner-

arbeit bespricht der Lehrer mit der Klasse die Lösungen.
Es kann auf die Kommaregelung und den Einsatz von Sprechpausen bei notwendigen und nicht notwendigen Relativsätzen hingewiesen werden: Nicht notwendige Relativsätze werden durch ein Komma bzw. eine Sprechpause vom übergeordneten Satz abgehoben. Bei notwendigen Relativsätzen erscheint weder ein Komma – im Gegensatz zum Deutschen – noch eine Sprechpause.

● Lösungen

Korrigierte Falschaussagen:

1. *'Thriller', made by Michael Jackson, is the world's best-selling album.*
4. *The smallest state in the world, populated by about 1000 people, is the Vatican City.*
5. *One of the world's most famous tourist spots is the Colosseum, built nearly 2000 years ago.*
7. *The most popular sport, played all over the world, is football.*
8. *The sport liked best by most Americans is baseball.*
9. *The scientist imprisoned for writing that the earth travels around the sun was Galileo.*
10. *The first man sent to the moon was a Russian.*
13. *The lowest temperature ever recorded was minus 89° C in Antarctica.*
16. *The language spoken by most people in the world is Chinese.*

Das in dieser Übung verwendete „Allerweltswissen" ist folgender, regelmäßig auf den neuesten Stand gebrachten und speziell für Jugendliche gedachten Veröffentlichung entnommen: Kay, Ann: Factfinder. London, Kingfisher Books 1987.

2. The changing world

In einem ersten Schritt trägt der Lehrer den Text "The changing world" laut vor. Die Lernenden versuchen, den Inhalt global zu erfassen. In einem zweiten Schritt lesen die Schüler den Text leise und versuchen, ihn mit Hilfe der auf dem Arbeitsblatt abgebildeten Illustrationen detailliert zu verstehen. In einem dritten Schritt vervollständigen sie die anschließende Textzusammenfassung unter Verwendung der entsprechenden Partizip Perfekt-Formen.

● Lösung

Pictures sent to earth by satellite show how the world is changing. Photos taken of the earth's atmosphere reveal that the ozone layer is disappearing. Satellite photos shown on TV have helped to raise awareness of this process, called/known as global warming. Global warming, caused by poisonous gases known as 'greenhouse gases', means that the atmosphere is becoming warmer. The atmosphere, no longer protected by the ozone layer, is being damaged by the sun's rays. Chemicals, used in sprays and fridges and also gases produced by traffic and industry are causing the greenhouse effect. These gases, trapped in the earth's atmosphere, stop the sun's heat from escaping. Reports written on global warming warn that polar ice, melted by the sun, would cause widespread flooding.

A 25

Partizipialkonstruktionen: satzverkürzend und als Adjektive

Diese Einheit beschäftigt sich schwerpunktmäßig mit Partizipialkonstruktionen, die sowohl mit *present participles* als auch *past participles* gebildet sind, und einerseits adverbiale Nebensätze ersetzen (*Then travel by coach into the countryside before getting off for a guided walk = before you get off ...*) and andererseits für Relativsätze eintreten können (*An attractive village set in horse-riding country = which is set ...*).
Partizipialkonstruktionen sind kürzer als vergleichbare Nebensätze, wirken geschliffener und prägnanter und kommen häufiger in der Schriftsprache und im förmlichen Stil vor. Als Textsorte für die vorliegende Einheit wurden informative Werbetexte gewählt, die die genannten Kriterien exemplarisch erfüllen.
Für die Werbesprache weiterhin typisch sind *present* und *past participles* in der Funktion attributiv und prädikativ gebrauchter Adjektive (*tea-making facilities, family run Guest House und Seaside House, situated close to town centre*). Diese Partizipialfügungen erscheinen in der zweiten Übung dieser Einheit.

1. The New Forest

Zunächst wird die im Südwesten der englischen Grafschaft Hampshire gelegene Wald-, Heide- und Moorlandschaft des *New Forest* auf einer Landkarte lokalisiert. Der *New Forest*, der einst das Jagdgebiet Wilhelm des Eroberers war, beherbergt heute noch alle drei Arten britischen Rotwilds und ist für seine ungezähmten Ponys berühmt. Im Jahre 1992 wurde das Gebiet zu einem Nationalpark erklärt.
Die Schüler versuchen, in Partner- oder Gruppenarbeit und mit Hilfe eines Wörterbuchs die einem offiziellen *New Forest*-Führer entnommenen authentischen Texte zu verstehen. Hingewiesen werden sollte auf die Aussprache von Beaulieu – ['bju:li].
Die auf die Texte folgende Übung verdeutlicht die Funktion der in ihnen verwendeten Partizipialkonstruktionen.

● Lösungen
1. *It is surrounded by – surrounded by (Lyndhurst)*
2. *It promotes – promoting (Forest Arts Centre)*
3. *It tells – telling (video)*
4. *It overlooks – overlooking (caravan park)*
5. *It is renowned for – renowned for (River Avon)*
6. *It includes – including (Calshot Activity Centre)*
7. *Before you get off – before getting off (coach)*
8. *It is best known for – best known for (Furzey)*
9. *It is displayed – displayed (work of local artists)*
10. *It is set – set (Burley)*
11. *Once you have discovered them – once discovered (hidden treasures)*
12. *It is situated on – situated on (caravan park)*

2. Hotels in Britain
Zunächst versuchen die Schüler, in Partner- oder Gruppenarbeit und mit Hilfe eines Wörterbuchs die authentischen Werbeanzeigen dreier britischer Hotels zu verstehen.
In der ersten nachfolgenden Übung transformieren die Schüler einige aus den Texten ausgewählten Partizipialkonstruktionen in Sätze mit finiten Verben, und in der zweiten Übung ordnen sie vorgegebenen Sätzen mit finiten Verben die in den Texten enthaltenen entsprechenden Partizipialkonstruktionen zu.

● Lösungen
1. *It has facilities to make tea*
2. *It is run by a family*
3. *It is/has been recommended internationally*
4. *It is/has been approved by the A.A.*
5. *These prices depend on the season*

Find participle constructions ... :
1. *offering*
2. *situated close to town centre*
3. *sleeping up to 6*
4. *conveniently situated for Dover Priory railway station*
5. *overlooking green park*
6. *A.A. listed*
7. *well-maintained secluded rear garden*

3. Writing an advertisement
Auf der Basis vorgegebener unverknüpfter Einzelsätze schreiben die Schüler eine dem Stil der Textsorte entsprechende, mit Partizipialkonstruktionen versehene Hotelwerbeanzeige.

● Vorgeschlagene Lösung
Run by the Bolton family, the Kingswood Hotel is a beautifully furnished small hotel.
Higly recommended and A.A. listed, it is personally managed by Lynne Bolton.
Situated close to the town centre, visitors can easily walk to the shops.
Overlooking the bay, we have wonderful views of the sea.
Set in large gardens, the hotel provides peaceful surroundings to simply relax.
Only a few miles away is the lovely New Forest, offering marvellous opportunities for walking and horse-riding.
A warm welcome, whether staying overnight or longer.
Terms: £ 35.00 B & B per person, depending on the season. Family rooms sleeping 4 from £ 70.

A 26

Have/get + Objekt + *past participle*

Übungen 1–4 beschäftigen sich mit der Struktur *to have/get something done* mit der Bedeutung „etwas machen lassen“. Übung 5 hingegen behandelt das Satzmuster *get* + Objekt + *past participle* im passivischen Sinn: das Subjekt ist die von einer unangenehmen Handlung betroffene Person, z.B. *She got her fingers burned. You'll get your bike stolen.*

1. Where would you go?
Die erste Übung kann folgendermaßen eingeführt werden:

L: *You can speak English quite well now. Sometime you might get a job in an English speaking country. If you lived there for a longer time there are a lot of things where you'd need expert help – you'd need to get a lot of things done for you. For example, you'd need to have your photos developed. And you might not have a washing machine. So you'd need to get your washing done somewhere. Let's see if you could find all the services you'd need.*

In Partnerarbeit stellen sich die Schüler abwechselnd die Fragen auf dem Arbeitsblatt:

S1: *Where would you go to have your watch repaired?*
S2: *To Grayson's. Where would you go to have your clothes cleaned?*
S1: *To ...*
usw.

● Lösungen
Where would you go to have
– *your hair cut? – Unisex hairdressing*
– *your coat cleaned? – Kleenit's*
– *your eyes tested? – MOONEY'S*
– *your shoes mended? – Hall's Heel Bar*
– *your photos developed? – NEEDHAM's*
– *your hair dyed? – Unisex hairdressing*
– *your washing done – THE LAUNDRETTE*
– *your glasses cleaned? – MOONEY'S*
– *your money changed? – NATIONAL WESTMINSTER BANK*
– *a passport photo taken? – NEEDHAM'S*

Which number would you ring to get
- *something typed? – 601548*
- *your fortune told? – 28556*
- *your room decorated? – 223066*
- *your teeth checked? – 529034*
- *your car serviced? – 984202*
- *your oven mended? – 83104*
- *your windows cleaned? – 443005*

2. What should they do?
In dieser für Partner- oder Gruppenarbeit gedachten Übung wird die Struktur in der dritten Person Singular und Plural verwendet. Die einzusetzenden Verben können der vorausgegangenen Übung entnommen werden.

● Lösungen
2. *He should have/get it cut.*
3. *She should have/get it dyed.*
4. *He should have/get it mended/repaired.*
5. *They should have/get it decorated.*
6. *He should have/get it cleaned.*
7. *She should have/get it serviced/checked/mended/ repaired.*
8. *She should have/get them cleaned.*
9. *She should have/get her ears/hearing tested.*
10. *He should have/get his eyes tested/checked.*

3. Have you ever had it done?
In Partnerarbeit stellen sich die Schüler gegenseitig Fragen nach dem Schema des angegebenen Musters und mit Hilfe des vorgeschlagenen Wortschatzes, z.B.

S1: *Have you ever had your fortune told?*
S2: *No. Have you?*
S1: *Yes, once/a few years ago/...*
S2: *Have you ever had your hair dyed?*
usw.

4. Jokes
In Gruppenarbeit versuchen die Schüler die Witze zu vervollständigen.
1. *Time to have/get the clock repaired.*
2. *And I want to have/get my bike mended and my violin broken.*

5. Warnings
● Lösungen
1. *You'll get it stolen.*
2. *You'll get your fingers burned/burnt.*
3. *Someone will get their windows broken.*
4. *You'll get your licence taken away.*

A 27

Partizip Präsens nach *need/want*

What needs doing?
Zur Einführung bringt der Lehrer einige Gegenstände mit, die reparaturbedürftig sind, z.B. kaputtes Spielzeug und zerrissene Kleidungsstücke. Die unterstrichenen Sätze werden an die Tafel bzw. auf den OHP geschrieben.

L: *Look at this toy. It's broken. It needs mending. And these socks have got holes in them. They want mending, too.*

Form und Bedeutung der Struktur werden zusammen mit den Schülern erarbeitet:

L: (Deutet auf die angeschriebenen Sätze) *Look, we can say 'something needs doing' or 'something wants doing'. What does this mean? How else could you say it?*

The socks want mending means: Someone should...?

S: *Mend the socks.*
L: (Ergänzt den Satz an der Tafel):
The socks want mending.
Someone should mend the socks.
L: *Now look at this picture* (Arbeitsblatt). *Can you see anything that wants mending in this room? What else wants doing?*

Mit Hilfe der im Merkkasten festgehaltenen Regel und des angegebenen Wortschatzes schreiben die Schüler in Partner- oder Einzelarbeit auf, was in dem auf dem Arbeitsblatt abgebildeten Zimmer alles getan werden muß.

● Lösungen
The room needs/wants tidying up.
The clothes need putting away.
The plants need watering.
The cupboard needs painting.
The waste-paper basket needs emptying.
The ash-tray needs emptying.
The bed needs making.
The lamp needs repairing.
The curtains need mending.
The pots need washing.
The carpet needs cleaning/hoovering.
The grass needs cutting.

A 28

Partizip Präsens als Ergänzung zum Verb

Das Partizip Präsens wird im Englischen häufig verwendet, um Begleit- oder Nebenumstände wiederzugeben. Die Konstruktion ist kürzer und wirkt geschliffener als zwei Hauptsätze oder eine Verbindung mit *and*, vgl.:

Colin is in his room doing his homework.
Colin is in his room. He is doing his homework.

Die *-ing* Form steht insbesondere nach Verben der Ruhe, z.B. *lie*, *stand* und *sit*, wie in Übung 2 verdeutlicht.

1. Could I speak to Colin, please?
Zur Einführung in die erste Übung zeichnet der Lehrer einige einfache Strichfiguren, die in einer bestimmten Umgebung eine bestimmte Handlung ausführen, z.B.:

John's in the living room watching TV.

Weitere Vorschläge:
... in the garden washing the car/mending her/his bike/ playing with the dog
... in her/his room reading/playing the guitar
... in the living room listening to the radio/music
... in the kitchen washing up/making a cup of tea/having her/his breakfast.

Das auf dem Arbeitsblatt abgebildete Mustertelefongespräch dient als Beispiel für die anschließende Partnerarbeit. Der Merkkasten erklärt Form und Bedeutung der Struktur.

In Partnerarbeit erstellen und üben die Schüler Telefongespräche nach dem vorgegebenen Muster. Ausgewählte Schüler können ihre Gespräche der Klasse vortragen.

2. Busy doing nothing
Die Auseinandersetzung der Familie Baxter wird in Einzel- oder Partnerarbeit schriftlich vervollständigt. Danach wird der Text zugedeckt, und die Schüler versuchen, die Minidialoge in Vierergruppen und ohne Hilfe der Vorlage nachzusprechen.

● Lösungen

Angela:	*I've been standing selling clothes all day.*
Mrs Baxter:	*Colin, you're only sitting watching TV.*
Mrs Baxter:	*Joe, you're just standing looking out of the window.*
Joe:	*He's been standing looking out of his window for about half an hour.*

A 29

Verben mit zwei Objekten

Mit diesem Arbeitsblatt werden Satzmuster mit direktem und indirektem Objekt wiederholt und geübt. Die Schüler sollen erkennen, daß sich die Reihenfolge der Objekte nach bestimmten Verben auf die Satzbedeutung auswirken kann: so steht gewöhnlich dasjenige Objekt an zweiter Stelle, das die meiste oder die wichtigste Information enthält.
Der Bedeutungsunterschied der beiden Satzmuster kann wie folgt in Erinnerung gerufen werden. Der Lehrer bringt mehrere kleine Gegenstände mit, die sich Schüler zuwerfen lassen, z.B. einen Ball, einen Radiergummi, einen Handschuh oder ein Taschentuch. Der Lehrer wirft den Schülern diese Gegenstände zu und kommentiert darauf seine Handlung, z.B. *I threw the ball to Andy und I threw the rubber to Barbara.*
Dann wird der Schwerpunkt auf die Gegenstände verlagert mit folgendem Kommentar des Lehrers: *What did I throw to Andy? The ball? The glove?* Die Schüler antworten mit dem natürlichen, verkürzten Satz: *The ball.* Der Lehrer nimmt die Antwort auf mit dem Kommentar: *Yes, you're right. I threw him the ball not the rubber.* Beide Satzmuster werden im Verlauf der Handlung an die Tafel geschrieben. Sie dienen den Schülern zur Erarbeitung einer groben Regel: „Was betont wird, steht am Schluß des Satzes".

1. What presents has Mrs Wilson bought?
Die erste Übung des Arbeitsblatts bezieht sich auf solche Fragen, die das direkte Objekt betonen: ***What*** *has Mrs. Wilson bought/got for Diane ...?*
Das Arbeitsblatt enthält eine Einkaufsliste mit Weihnachtsgeschenken. Bei zugedeckten Arbeitsblättern wird der erste Posten der Liste auf zwei verschiedene Arten vom Lehrer verbalisiert: *Mrs Wilson has bought a video for Ken* und *She has bought Ken a video.* Die Schüler werden aufgefordert, die unterschiedliche Aussagekraft der beiden Sätze zu beschreiben (Betonung auf der Person im ersten Satz und Betonung eher auf dem Geschenk im zweiten). Die Schüler vergleichen ihre Vermutungen mit dem Merkkasten auf dem Arbeitsblatt.

Was fällt dir bei Satz 2 auf?
Die Aufmerksamkeit wird auf den Wegfall der Präposition *for* im zweiten Satz gelenkt. Die Präpositionen fallen in den folgenden Fällen auch bei *get* und *give* weg: *She has* ***got Ken*** *a video; she is going to* ***give Ken*** *a video.*

A 29

● Lösungen

1. *She has bought Diane a camera.*
2. *She has bought Tony a game.*

1. *She has got Laura a book.*
2. *She has got Alan a watch.*
3. *She has got Barbara a scarf.*

1. *She is going to give Mary a ring.*
2. *She is going to give Wayne a football.*
3. *She is going to give Josie a necklace.*

2. Who are the presents for?

Die Struktur Verb + direktes Objekt + Präposition + indirektes Objekt wird mittels eines Gedächtnisspiels, in dem sich die Schüler an die beschenkten Personen erinnern müssen, geübt. Das Arbeitsblatt wird so abgedeckt, daß nur die abgebildeten Geschenke sichtbar bleiben. Die Schüler versuchen, diese aus dem Gedächtnis den beschenkten Personen zuzuordnen. Dabei sollen sie zwischen den drei angebotenen Strukturen variieren:

She has bought the ... for ...
She has got the ... for ...
She is going to give the ... to ...

3. Birthdays

Das Thema „Geschenke" wird erweitert, indem die Schüler aufgefordert werden, ihr eigenes Geschenkverhalten zu reflektieren. Mit Hilfe der die beiden Satzmuster enthaltenden, auf dem Arbeitsblatt vorgegebenen Strukturen berichten sie im Klassenverband, welche Art von Geschenken sie üblicherweise kaufen (*I usually get (my mother) a/some ...*), welche Geschenke sie schon gekauft bzw. selbst gemacht haben (*Last year/Once I bought/gave/got/made/sent ...*), und wie die Empfänger darauf reagierten (*He loved it/didn't like it much*). Sie können sich auch Gedanken über zukünftige Geschenke machen (*This year I think I'll/might buy/get/give ...*). Zur Festigung schreiben die Schüler einige ihrer Gedanken auf, z. B.

- *I'd like to give/get/buy/make my ... a/some ...*
- *I think I'll (get) a/some ... for my ...*
- *Last year I ... my ... a/some ...*
- *Once I ... a/some for my ...*
  He/She liked .../didn't ...

4. Show me your presents

Die beiden Satzmuster dieser Einheit werden nun in Verbindung mit Personalpronomen und den Verben *lend, play, read* und *show* geübt. Die Schüler spekulieren mit Hilfe von Lückentexten darüber, wie Dritte auf die in Übung 1 genannten Weihnachtsgeschenke reagieren könnten. Die Lückentexte können mit oder ohne Rückgriff auf Übung 1 – in letzterem Fall also als Gedächtnisübung – vervollständigt werden. Da drei der Fragen von Einzelpersonen und zwei von Paaren gestellt werden, müssen die Schüler zwischen den Personalpronomen *me* und *us* wählen.

● Lösungen

Tracy: *"Will you lend/show me your camera, Diane?"*
Ann: *"Will you lend/show/read me your new book, Laura?"*
Derek and Lynne: *"Will you/show/lend us your new game, Tony?"*
Suzy: *"Will you show/lend me your scarf, Barbara?"*
Wayne and Maria: *"Will you play/lend us your new video, Ken?"*

Diane's mother asks her daughter

Abweichend von dem Satzmuster der fünf vorausgegangenen Fragen wird nun das Satzmuster Verb + direktes Objekt + Präposition + indirektes Objekt geübt.

● Lösungen

"Have you showed your (new) video to your father?"
"You could read your new book to your sister."

Die unterschiedliche Funktion der beiden Strukturen wird anschließend zusammen mit den Lernenden erarbeitet.

● Lösungen

In Sätze des Typs 1 wird das Augenmerk auf die Gegenstände gerichtet, in Sätzen des Typs 2 eher auf die Person.

Folgender Zungenbrecher dient als lustiger Merksatz für die beiden Strukturen:

Say five times:
Suzy showed Sue her shoe.
Suzy showed her shoe to Sue.

Zum Abschluß können die Schüler versuchen, folgenden Witz zu erklären:

Jimmy: *Do you sell dogs' meat?*
Butcher: *Only if they're with an adult.*

Jimmy fragt nach Fleisch als Futter für seinen Hund. Der Metzger versteht die Frage jedoch falsch, nämlich: „Verkaufen Sie Fleisch an Hunde?", d.h. *Do you sell dogs* (ohne Genitivapostroph) *meat?* oder eindeutiger *Do you sell meat to dogs?*

5. Tell me, please

Besondere Schwierigkeiten für deutsche Schüler bildet die richtige syntaktische Verwendung der Verben *explain, say* und *tell.*

Die Schüler vervollständigen die Lückensätze und können dazu die Regeln im anschließenden Merkkasten zu Hilfe nehmen.

● Lösungen
They ask him, "Can you tell us how to play?"
Tony said that he couldn't play it himself yet.

Folgende Merksätze für den Unterschied zwischen say und tell sind hilfreich:
Tell me what you said.
You told me you wouldn't say a word.
I said I wouldn't tell anyone.

A 30

Adverbien der Zeit; Präpositionen

Dieses Arbeitsblatt beschäftigt sich mit adverbialen Ausdrücken der Zeit, ihrer Stellung im Satz (Übungen 1–3), ihrer Stellung untereinander (Übung 4) und mit den in ihnen verwendeten Präpositionen (Übung 5). Als Themen, für deren Versprachlichung Zeitadverbien repräsentativ verwendet werden, kommen besonders kulturelle Feste in Frage – in dieser Einheit „Das chinesische Neue Jahr" und „Weihnachten in Großbritannien" –, als Textsorten Features in Zeitungen und Zeitschriften.

1. The Chinese New Year
Das Thema läßt sich durch ein kurzes Gespräch über das Feiern von Festen im allgemeinen einführen, z.B.
L: *Is it anybody's birthday today? Next week? The week after? Are you going to have a party?*
When do you all have parties – for your birthdays? At Christmas?
S: *On New Year's Eve/...*
An dieser Stelle kann schon vorhandenes Wissen über Weihnachten oder Neujahr in anderen Ländern gesammelt werden. *Do you know how people celebrate Christmas or New Year in other countries?*
Nach der Einführung liest der Lehrer den Text *The Chinese New Year* vor, wobei die Schüler noch nicht mitlesen.

2. Time expressions
Die Schüler lesen den Text leise, unterstreichen die Zeitadverbien und versuchen, eine Regel über deren Stellung im Satz zu bilden. Der Merkkasten kann zu Hilfe gezogen werden.

● Lösungen
Between 21 January and 19 February, for two weeks, one week before the New Years starts, in the last year, on the evening before New Year, at New Year, on New Year's Day, years ago, in 1994, towards the end of the celebrations, during the Cultural Revolution, in the 1980s, today.

3. Can you explain how the Chinese celebrate the New Year?
Zur Festigung des Gebrauchs und der Stellung der Zeitadverbien ordnen die Schüler in Gruppen- oder Partnerarbeit die in zwei Spalten abgedruckten Satzanfänge und -enden einander zu.

● Lösungsvorschlag
The Chinese New Year starts sometime in January or February.
The celebrations last for a couple of weeks.
A week before the New Year starts the family honour the kitchen god.
Then he goes to Heaven to report on the family.
He is welcomed back the evening before New Year.
At New Year people only eat vegetarian meals.
On New Year's Day street festivals are held.
Years ago fireworks were very important.
But in 1994 they were banned.
Towards the end of the celebrations lanterns are hung up.
Religious traditions were banned during the Cultural Revolution.
But in the 1980s New Year celebrations started again.
Today many young Chinese prefer the Western style New Year.

An dieser Stelle bietet sich ein kurzes Wiederholen von Datumsangaben an:
1. Mehrere Schreibweisen:
January 17th 1943 — *17th January 1943*
December 2nd, 1996 — *2nd December, 1996*
Folgende Schreibweisen werden immer häufiger:
December 2, 1996 — *2 December 1996*

2. Abgekürzte Schreibweisen:
17/1/43 oder 17. 1. 43 = 17th January 1943
(Britisches Englisch)
1/17/43 oder 1. 17. 43 = January 17, 1943
(Amerikanisches Englisch)

3. Abgekürzte Monatsnamen:
January – Jan., February – Feb., March – Mar., April – Apr., August – Aug., September – Sept., October – Oct., November – Nov., December – Dec.

4. Mehrere Sprechweisen:
Britisches Englisch: *January the seventeenth* oder *the seventeenth of January.*
Amerikanisches Englisch: *January seventeenth* (Diese Form wird im britischen Englisch immer häufiger.)

4. A British Christmas
Die Reihenfolge mehrerer aufeinanderfolgender Zeitadverbien wird geübt, indem aus durcheinandergewürfelten Satzteilen zum Thema *A British Christmas* ein zusammenhängender Text rekonstruiert wird.

● Lösung
Lots of British people have Christmas parties. They start at about seven on Christmas Eve and often go on until early on Christmas Day, that is 25 December. Children wake up very early on Christmas morning. They open the presents that Father Christmas brought them the night before. Adults give each other presents after breakfast on Christmas morning. At about one o'clock on Christmas Day there is a huge Christmas dinner. Then, at three in the afternoon, most people listen to the Queen's Speech on television.

5. Talking about time: at – in – on?
● Lösungen
At Christmas, in December, on 25 December, on New Year's Eve, in the evening, at lunch-time, in the winter, on Wednesday evening, in 1998, at night, on my birthday, at half past five, at/on (AE) the weekend.

Nach dieser kurzen Wiederholung können die Lernenden versuchen, selbst eine Regel zu finden: *Get into groups and put these expressions into three lists: at – in – on. Can you find rules for when we use each preposition?*

● Lösung
at
- *for exact times: at 6.00 p.m., at three o'clock, (in informal English 'at' is usually dropped in expressions of time: What time are you coming? Three o'clock), at the moment*
- *for weekends: at the weekend (AE: on the weekend)*
- *for the whole of a public holiday: at Christmas, at New Year, at Easter*
- *for meals and mealtimes: at breakfast, at lunch-time*

in
- *for longer periods, e.g. parts of the day (except 'at night'): in the afternoon. (For a specific morning, type of morning, afternooen etc. we use 'on': I'll see you on Monday morning/On a sunny morning I like to go for a walk)*
- *for months, seasons, years and centuries: in December, in the spring, in 1066, in the twentieth century*
- *to say how soon something will happen: I'll ring you in two or three days; We'll have finished in about two weeks' time*
- *to say how long something takes to happen: She can run 200 metres in about 22 seconds*

on
- *for particular days, also particular days of a public holiday: on Saturday, on Tuesday afternoon, (In AE 'on' can be dropped before days of the week: I'll see you (on) Wednesday evening), on my birthday, on Christmas Day, on New Year's Eve, on Easter Monday*
- *for dates: on 25 December.*

6. Your Christmas and New Year
Nach einem kurzen Gespräch über Weihnachten in Deutschland können Schüler einen für eine Meinungsumfrage geeigneten Fragebogen zur Problematik der Kommerzialisierung des Weihnachtsfestes erstellen, z.B. *How do you usually spend Christmas? What do you think about Christmas? What would you change about it? Imagine an alternative Christmas. What would you give to someone who 'has everything'?* usw.

A 31

Adverbien des Ortes, der Richtung und der Zeit

Dieses Arbeitsblatt beschäftigt sich schwerpunktmäßig mit Adverbien und adverbialen Gruppen des Ortes und der Richtung und weniger ausführlich mit Adverbien der Zeit.
Als Textsorte eignet sich besonders der Wetterbericht, dessen wesentliche Bestandteile diese Strukturen ausmachen.
In den Übungen 1–4 werden Adverbien des Ortes und der Richtung sowie deren Stellung im Satz geübt. Übung 5 bietet eine kurze Wiederholung der relativen Stellung von Adverbien des Ortes und der Richtung einerseits und Adverbien der Zeit andererseits.

1. The weather forecast
Mit der Frage, ob schon jemand eine englischsprachige Fernsehsendung (z.B. Sky News oder CNN) gesehen oder einem englischen Radiosender (z.B. BBC, Radio 4) zugehört hat, wird an die Thematik des Wetterberichts herangeführt, z.B.

L: *Who has satellite TV at home? Can any of you receive an English speaking TV or radio channel? Have you ever watched Sky News, for instance, or CNN or listened to a British radio programme? There's one thing that people usually watch or listen to when they're planning their day. Do you know what I mean?*
S: *What's „Wetterbericht" in English?*

Nach dieser Einführung wird der Text unter Klärung etwaiger Verständnisschwierigkeiten still gelesen.

A 31

2. Talking about the weather
Zur Übung neuer und Aktivierung schon bekannter Adverbien des Ortes und der Richtung erstellen die Schüler in Einzel- oder Partnerarbeit eine neue Version des Textes. Dazu ersetzen sie die im Ausgangstext unterstrichenen Adverbien durch sinnentsprechende andere und tragen sie in den Lückentext ein.

● Lösung
Es gibt verschiedene Lösungsmöglichkeiten, z.B.:
It's a lovely morning where I am. In other parts of Britain, however, things aren't so good. Rain is coming into Scotland, and it will move towards the East coast. By midday it will probably be raining everywhere in Scotland. In the afternoon the sun might even come through in some places in Scotland.
At the moment it is raining hard around Manchester, but they might see a little sunshine here and there by mid-morning. By the afternoon it will be raining in most (parts) of the North. So if you don't have to go out today it's best to stay indoors/inside.
In most (parts) of the South it's a lovely sunny morning. This afternoon there may be a few showers in some parts/places/areas, but they will soon clear up. The best weather will be in the South-East area.

3. Adverbs of place and direction
Weitere Beispiele für Adverbien des Ortes und der Richtung werden in Partner- oder Gruppenarbeit sowohl dem Text als auch dem Schülerwortschatz entnommen. Denkbar ist auch ein zeitlich limitierter Wettbewerb:
Which group can think of the most
a) adverbs of place starting with at/in/on + noun.
b) adverbs of direction starting with go, come, walk.

● Lösungsvorschläge
Adverbs of place:
In the rest of the country, over Scotland (kann auch als Adverb der Richtung interpretiert werden), all over Scotland, here and there, in the Manchester area, between the showers, practically everywhere in the North, inside, down in the South, in most places, around the South-East, along the South coast, in the South-West, in most parts of the country, in some parts of Scotland, in the North and Central England, between, above.
Weitere Beispiele:
across (the street)/behind/beneath/over (the bridge)/half-way up, down/under
at school/work
at the cinema/baker's/door/traffic lights/corner/beginning/top/back
in bed/hospital/town
in the room/street/country/middle/newspaper
on holiday/top of/TV
on the table/wall/floor/board/bus/left of/radio/phone usw.

Adverbs of direction:
moving in from Ireland, move half-way across the country, go anywhere, disappear behind the clouds, travel around, move up the coast
Weitere Beispiele:
come in(to), come round; fall down; go away/behind/down/out/to/towards/through/under/up; run backwards and forwards; walk across/along/up and down/over (the bridge) usw.

4. Position of adverbs of place and direction
Anhand des Wetterberichts versuchen die Schüler, Regeln für die Stellung von Adverbien des Ortes und der Richtung im Satz zu finden.

● Lösungen
Adverbien des Ortes und der Richtung stehen meistens am Ende eines Satzes bzw. einer Sinngruppe, z.B. … here in London, … eastwards, … all over Scotland. Stehen sie am Satzanfang, habe sie die Funktion, einen Kontrast hervorzuheben, z.B. … here in London. In the rest of the country, however, … ; Down in the South (Kontrast zum Norden); In some parts of Scotland (Kontrast zu in most parts of the country); In the North and Central England (im Gegensatz zu Scotland); And in the South (Kontrast zu North and Central England).

Anmerkung:
Wenn auf adverbiale Gruppen in Satzanfangsstellung wie z.B. *Across the river, outside the house* etc. intransitive Verben wie *come, lie, stand, walk* etc. folgen, muß eine Inversion von Subjekt und Vollverb vorgenommen werden:
Across the river lies the town of Henley.
Outside the house stood a small boy.
Eine Verneinung mit *do/did* ist ausgeschlossen.

Adverbien der Richtung stehen meistens vor Adverbien des Ortes:
coming in – over Scotland; come through – here and there; moving in – from Ireland

● Lösung
1. *My penfriend lives in a small town in Wales.*
2. *Let's meet at the bus stop outside the town hall.*
Genaue Angaben stehen meistens vor weniger genauen.

Anmerkung:
Treffen mehrere verschieden lange Adverbien des Ortes aufeinander, so gilt die Regel kurz vor lang, z.B. *I'll see you in town – at the bus stop – on the corner of High Street.*

5. Position of adverbs of place, direction and time
Durch die Rekonstruktion durcheinandergewürfelter Satzteile zu Sätzen wird die Stellung der Adverbien des Ortes, der Richtung und der Zeit untereinander geübt.

● Lösungen
1. *It is lovely here in London this morning.*
2. *Rain will move eastwards later today.*
3. *It will be raining all over Scotland by midday.*
4. *Temperatures will drop to below freezing in some places tomorrow.*

Adverbien des Ortes und der Richtung stehen meistens vor Adverbien der Zeit.

A 32

Adjektiv oder Adverb?

In diesem Arbeitsblatt werden die folgenden Adverbien im Vergleich zu den dazu gehörenden Adjektiven und kontrastiv zum Deutschen geübt:
1. Adverbien, die von Adjektiven mit der Endung *-ly* abgeleitet sind, wie z.B. *careful, easy, bad, quick, slow, comfortable, fashionable*, und das zu *good* gehörende Adverb *well* (Übungen 1, 2, 6).
2. Adverbien und Adjektive mit gleicher Form und Bedeutung, z.B. *fast, early* (Übungen 1, 2, 6).
3. Adverbien mit gleicher Form und Bedeutung wie die dazu gehörenden Ajektive, z.B. Life *is hard; You work hard*, und Adverbien mit der Endung *-ly* und einer anderen Bedeutung, z.B. *You work hard; You've hardly got any money* (Übungen 1, 4, 5, 6).

Die abschließende siebte Übung geht auf Verben der sinnlichen Wahrnehmung ein, nach denen Adjektive und nicht Adverbien stehen, wie z.B. *look, feel, taste, smell, sound.*

1. What are they like?
Mit Hilfe von Vorgaben, in denen in Form eines Überblicks alle oben angeführten Typen von Adverbien verwendet werden, befragen sich die Schüler gegenseitig in Partnerarbeit.
Daran anschließend geben ausgewählte Schüler mündlich oder schriftlich nach dem vorgegebenen Muster der Klasse einen Bericht über ihre Gesprächspartner.

2. German and English
Eine Übersetzung aus dem Deutschen ins Englische macht kontrastiv die Besonderheiten englischer Adverbien bewußt.

● Lösungen
1. a) *Anna is careful.*
   b) *Anna works carefully.*
2. a) *Paul is a good football player.*
   b) *Paul plays football well.*
3. a) *a fast car*
   b) *to drive fast*
4. a) *in the early morning*
   b) *to get up early*

Im Deutschen haben Adjektiv und Adverb die gleiche Form, im Englischen nur manchmal.

Vervollständige diese Regeln durch Beispiele:
Durch das Vervollständigen dreier Regeln festigen die Schüler ihre grammatischen Kenntnisse.

● Lösungen
Viele Adverbien werden mit der Endung *-ly* von Adjektiven abgeleitet, z.B. *carefull, easy, bad, quick, slow, comfortable, fashionable* usw.
Die Adverbform von *good* ist *well.*
Manche Adjektive und Adverbien haben gleiche Form und gleiche Bedeutung z.B. *fast, early, (hard, late* – vgl. Übungen 4 und 5).

Weitere Beispiele: *daily, weekly, the daily paper arrives at six/The paper arrives daily at six.*

3. Adjectives with two adverb forms: hard, late, high, near
Ein Werbeplakat, ein Kurzdialog und ins Deutsche zu übersetzende Sätze verdeutlichen die verschiedenen Funktionen und Bedeutungen von *hard/hardly, late/lately, high/highly,* und *near/nearly.*

● Lösungen
Adjektiv: Life is hard?
Adverb: You work hard, but you've hardly got any money?

Adjektiv: ... it's late; a later one
Adverb: I haven't seen you lately; arrive late

1. *hoch*
2. *hoch/höchst intelligent; hoch (bezahlt)*
3. *nah*
4., 5. *beinahe*

Ein Regelkasten faßt die gewonnenen grammatischen Erkenntnisse zusammen.

4. Hardly (ever, any)
Mit Hilfe einer Umformungsaufgabe und analog zu dem vorgegebenen Beispiel üben die Schüler Form und Funktion von *hardly, hardly ever* und *hardly any.*

A 32

● Lösungen

1. *I hardly ever watch TV.*
2. *I can hardly read your writing.*
3. *Helen hardly said anything to me.*
4. *We've hardly any biscuits left.*
5. *Hardly anyone passed the exam.*
6. *Diane hardly eats anything.*
7. *Grandad hardly ever goes out.*

5. School reports

Alle bis zu diesem Zeitpunkt verwendeten Arten von Adverbien werden zusammengefaßt und durch Vervollständigen eines Lückentextes geübt.

● Lösungen

Lisa learns quickly, but she works carelessly. She does things too fast. She hardly ever does her homework. She often arrives/is often late for school, although lately she has been improving.
She is a very popular girl and finds it easy to make friends. She also draws very well.

Simon is a quick learner. He is a careful, fast worker. He is never late for school.
He is rather lonely and does not make friends easily. He is a good violinist.

6. Describing things

Mit Hilfe einer Zuordnungsaufgabe üben die Schüler, daß nach Verben der sinnlichen Wahrnehmung ein Adjektiv und kein Adverb folgt.

● Lösungen

It often tastes horrible – medicine
It tastes sweet – honey
It smells lovely – fresh bread
They smell awful – old socks
It looks beautiful – new snow
They look soft - cats
it feels cold – ice
It feels sharp – a needle
They sound terrible – bagpipes

Nach dem vorgegebenen Muster schreiben die Schüler mehrere eigene Sätze.
Beispiele:

It tastes lovely and it smells great – a hot dog.
They smell wonderful and look beautiful – flowers.

WEITERE TITEL ZUR UNTERRICHTSVORBEREITUNG

ENGLISCH

von Ziegésar,
Detlef und Margaret
Arbeitsblätter
Englische Grammatik
5./6. Schuljahr
43 Arbeitsblätter für einen kommunikativen Grammatikunterricht
ISBN 3-12-927874-5

von Ziegésar,
Detlef und Margaret
Arbeitsblätter
Englische Grammatik
7./8. Schuljahr
34 Arbeitsblätter für einen kommunikativen Grammatikunterricht
ISBN 3-12-927875-3

von Ziegésar,
Detlef und Margaret
Arbeitsblätter
Englische Grammatik
9./10. Schuljahr
27 Arbeitsblätter für einen kommunikativen Grammatikunterricht
ISBN 3-12-927884-2

Pulm, Manfred/
Röhrig, Johannes
Unterrichtsideen
Textarbeit im Englischunterricht der Sekundarstufe II
Didaktische Kommentare und methodische Anregungen zum Themenbereich Cross-cultural Encounters
ISBN 3-12-922694-X

Benecke, Ingrid
Stundenblätter
„Macbeth"
Sekundarstufe II
ISBN 3-12-925165-0

Hoops, Traudl/
Hoops, Wiklef
Stundenblätter
Salinger „The Catcher in the Rye"
Sekundarstufe II
ISBN 3-12-925131-6

Kaiser, Gerd
Stundenblätter
Golding „Lord of the Flies"
Sekundarstufe II
ISBN 3-12-925162-6

Kaiser, Gerd
Stundenblätter
Hemmingway „Short Stories"
Sekundarstufe II
ISBN 3-12-925151-0

Petruschke, Adelheid/
Rösner, Angelika
Stundenblätter
Lyrische Texte im Englischunterricht
Sekundarstufe II
ISBN 3-12-925192-8

Rimmelspacher-Heuseler, Frauke
Stundenblätter
Miller „Death of a Salesman"
Sekundarstufe II
ISBN 3-12-925191-X

Sonnhüter, Ingrid
Stundenblätter
Aldous Huxley „Brave New World"
Sekundarstufe II
ISBN 3-12-925111-1

Alle Titel der Reihen Interpretationshilfen, Arbeitsblätter, Stundenblätter und Unterrichtsideen finden Sie im Schulpraxiskatalog Nr. P710217.
Fragen Sie Ihren Buchhändler oder bestellen Sie ihn kostenlos direkt bei uns.

ISBN 3-12-927415-4ISBN 3-12-927414-6ISBN 3-12-922675-3ISBN 3-12-922654-0ISBN 3-12-922672-9ISBN 3-12-922711-3ISBN 3-12-922681-8ISBN 3-12-922661-3ISBN 3-12-922602-8ISBN 3-12-922606-0ISBN 3-12-922605-2